THE THREE-MINUTE CLASSROOM WALK-THROUGH

The THREE-MINUTE CLASSROOM WALK-THROUGH

CHANGING SCHOOL
SUPERVISORY PRACTICE
ONE TEACHER AT A TIME

CAROLYN J. DOWNEY

BETTY E. STEFFY • FENWICK W. ENGLISH

LARRY E. FRASE • WILLIAM K. POSTON, JR.

CORWIN PRESS
A Sage Publications Company
Thousand Oaks, California

For information:

Corwin Press
A Sage Publications Company
2455 Teller Road
Thousand Oaks, California 91320
www.corwiDnpress.com

Sage Publications Ltd
1 Oliver's Yard
55 City Road
London EC1Y 1SP
United Kingdom

Sage Publications India Pvt. Ltd.
B-42, Panchsheel Enclave
Post Box 4109
New Delhi 110 017 India

Printed in the United States of America

Library of Congress Cataloging-in-Publication Data

The three-minute classroom walk-through : changing school supervisory practice one teacher at a time / by Carolyn J. Downey . . . [et al.].
    p. cm.
Includes bibliographical references and index.
    ISBN 978-0-7619-2966-6 (cloth) --- ISBN 978-0-7619-2967-3
1. School supervision. 2. Teacher-principal relationships. 3. Observation (Educational method) 4. Reflection (Philosophy) I. Downey, Carolyn J.
LB2806.4.T57 2004 371.2′03—dc22

                                        2003026985

This book is printed on acid-free paper.

                07   08   10   9   8

Acquisitions Editor:	Robert D. Clouse
Editorial Assistant:	Jingle Vea
Production Editor:	Kristen Gibson
Copy Editor:	Teresa Herlinger
Typesetter:	C&M Digitals (P) Ltd.
Indexer:	Naomi Linzer
Proofreader:	Kris Bergstad
Cover Designer:	Anthony Paular

Contents

Preface   viii

About the Authors   xiii

**1. Understanding the Rationale Underlying the
   Walk-Through and Reflective Practice Approach**   1

   What Is the Downey Walk-Through?   2

   Why Walk-Throughs?   5

   The Evolution of the Downey Walk-Through Process   9

**2. Conducting the Walk-Through Observation:
   A Five-Step Process**   17

   The Five-Step Observation Structure   20

   Step 1: Student Orientation to Work   21

   Step 2: Curricular Decision Points   23

   Step 3: Instructional Decision Points   33

   Step 4: "Walk the Walls"–Curricular
       and Instructional Decisions   35

   Step 5: Safety and Health Issues   36

   Summary   41

**3. Moving Staff to Reflective Inquiry: Focusing
   on the Reflective Question and Conversation**   43

   How Do We Provide Direct Feedback?   45

   How Do We Provide Indirect Opportunities for
       Reflective Inquiry?   57

   How Do We Ask Reflective Questions and Carry
       on the Conversation?   60

   The Reflective Question   61

   The Reflective Conversation   75

   Cautions in Using the Reflective Question
       and Conversation   78

4. **Constructing a Taxonomy of Reflective Questions and Their Use in the Classroom Walk-Through** 83

    The Novice/Apprentice 85

    The Professional Teacher 86

    The Expert Teacher 86

    Limitations of the Taxonomy 97

5. **Establishing Logistical Procedures for Implementing the Walk-Through Process** 99

    Finding the Time 99

    Preparing Staff, Students, and Parents 101

    Record Keeping 105

    Board Policy to Support Walk-Throughs 107

6. **Cultivating the Culture: Effectuating Change That Works** 109

    Lessons Learned About Change in Educational Cultures 110

    Challenges and Barriers to Change 112

    Deciding When to Intervene: The Marginal Teacher 114

    Examples of Successful Implementation: Making the Walk-Through Process Work 116

    Cultivating the Culture: A Final Word 123

7. **Using the Walk-Through Process to Promote a Collaborative, Reflective Culture** 125

    Early History 126

    Developmental Supervision and Mentoring 131

    The Teacher as an Adult Learner 134

    Promoting Development 137

8. **Determining Whether Walk-Throughs Are the Right Stuff** 141

    Background and History of Management by Wandering Around 143

    Why Are Both a Research and a Theory Base Needed Before Adopting an Innovation? 145

    The MBWA Research Results 148

    The Walk-Through With Reflective Question Research 155

**9. Understanding the Walk-Through
   as a Discursive Practice**   159
   Examining the Dimensions of the Walk-Through   163
   Changing the Discursive Practice of "Corrective"
      Supervision   164
   Some Issues With the Model   166
   A Pause to Consider Your Specific Situation   170
   Troubleshooting Problems With
      the Downey Walk-Through   171
   Summary   173

**10. Linking the Walk-Through Process to a Model
   of Teacher Growth**   175
   Walk-Throughs and the Teacher Growth Model   176
   The Model   177
   Transformative Learning as It Relates to the Model   181
   Organizational Learning and Transformation   181
   Providing Feedback Conversation for Growth   184

References   187

Index   195

Preface

The approach to the classroom walk-throughs presented in this book was created by Carolyn Downey. It is unique. It redefines the professional relationships of classroom supervisory practice, it changes the language of the discourse itself by focusing on the relationships between teachers and principals, and it emphasizes a different level of content analysis regarding classroom work. It puts into practice the vision of what supervision should be, a vision that can be traced back to its early beginnings in the 1600s. While Downey's vision has been realized in isolated schools, it has yet to be reflected in the practices of the field as a whole. More than a model of principal-teacher interaction, the Downey approach is about changing an entire school culture.

It is because of the distinctiveness of this vision that we determined to write a book to more sharply differentiate its premises and potential. We wanted to (1) provide a source for a greater explanation of the approach to classroom walk-throughs created by Carolyn Downey; (2) establish greater clarity as to why this approach is preferred over others that lead to teacher growth and renewal and improved student achievement for all; and (3) provide an expanded contextual framework for the practice of instructional supervision, which is often void of any curricular linkages to larger organizational purposes. Too often in the past, teaching effectiveness was characterized as "curriculum-free" when, in fact, teachers are employed to teach state-adopted and locally approved curriculum content.

The Downey approach actually changes how principals approach supervision. In reality, we don't like what the term *supervision* has come to mean because it often smacks of a heritage of superior-subordinate relationships that hinder improved professional practice for educators, who require greater autonomy in their work, and it has a long history of gender discrimination in the public schools (see Blount, 1999; Shakeshaft, 1989).

By definition, supervision of teachers has been one of the classic responsibilities of principals and supervisors in the schools over many decades (Tanner & Tanner, 1987). Such supervision was the foundation of historic roles in administration such as the old-time, male, county super-intendent who often rode on horseback over miles of unpaved roads to visit and "supervise" mostly female teachers in rural, one-room schools.

There can be little doubt that early exemplars of school supervision were based on industrial models. The long lines of gears, wheels, and conveyor belts punctuating the New England textile mills, which were teeming with gaggles of underpaid female workers arranged in rows, made it easier for the male shop foreman to oversee the work, point out deficiencies, and engage in immediate "corrective" actions. To a very great extent, such models are still common in the sweatshops of Third World countries where women and children still sew clothes today. There can be little doubt that the creation of the graded school was a mirror of the tex-tile mills, with its rows of classrooms arranged next to one other, and the underpaid, half-educated female teachers working among very large groups of students and being "supervised" by male principals. Efficiency has been the watchword in supervision for a long while. The legacy of scientific management typified by Frederick Taylor's clipboards and stop-watch can still be found lingering in proposals outlining alternative and cheaper forms of schooling.

This is the shadow heritage of school supervision, an unsavory lineage that still lingers in the hallways and classrooms of many contemporary schools. Though the rhetoric has been tailored to fit in with the newer, softer forms of managerial practices that emphasize "caring" and/or "collaboration," the model of managerial control—and with it the inevitable "parent-child" relationship between principals and teachers—often remains firmly intact. This is why the word *evaluation* is a polyvalent term; that is, it contains many meanings and the secondary ones may have eclipsed the one intended. Evaluation is often not only ineffective, it is also feared by legions of teachers because it is frequently mindless, unhelpful, and punitive. Good rarely ever comes from it and many injurious results may accrue, which can lead to more work instead of improved work.

The Downey approach to classroom walk-throughs is situated on a different axis. It rejects the superior-subordinate hegemony of principals and teachers that is often swathed in covert gender discrimination and replaces it with a collegial, egalitarian model of professional practice. It is centered on an adult-to-adult model of discourse that involves profes-sional conversation about practice. It rejects the "gotcha" model of inspec-tion where the principal or supervisor is looking for "what's wrong with this picture" and that is based on checklists and mindless conformity to contextless classroom practices. It replaces the infrequent, formal "dipstick" model of evaluation with very frequent, short, informal exchanges between principals and teachers. These short exchanges are considered an ongoing and integral part of reflective teaching practice— a practice that is *paperless*, because it is a continuing conversation over time.

In short, the Downey approach to classroom walk-throughs sheds the ghosts of factory models and relationships and re-centers professional practice on a new axis, one embodied in the vision of what supervision was supposed to accomplish in the first place. It recognizes that part and parcel of classroom practice is the relationship of the teacher to the person supervising him or her, as well as the teacher's relationships with students, parents, and other teachers. Everything in schools *is relational,* and never static. In this sense, the Downey model is not only fluid, moving, and dynamic—it is *antibureaucratic,* something that we will comment on later. This model is at odds with many bureaucratic practices that are not conducive to professional relationships that should rest on trust, fairness, egalitarianism, and autonomy between independent parties. The setting in which many teachers work is antiprofessional (beyond *un*professional).

So the Downey model is not just a model of supervisory practice that "fits" into bureaucratically organized schools; it is a model of changed relationships that will come to characterize an entire school. It is a way of developing a network of relationships as opposed to merely changing the principal-teacher dyad. In this sense, it is *radical.* It is this characteristic of the Downey approach that promises to alter the entire school climate and create a culture of high work performance for an entire school. This approach is about changing schools, one teacher at a time. That's the only way the change is ever permanent.

This book is divided into two parts. The first part, Chapters 1 through 6, describes the pragmatics of our approach to walk-throughs from its early conceptualization to the development of the step-by-step process of collecting information from short classroom visits and using this information to engage in reflective dialogue with teachers. This part concludes with suggestions for implementing the process and describes examples of successful implementation of the model in a variety of settings. The second part of the book, Chapters 7 through 10, takes a longer view and explores the historical development of supervision, reviews the research base for the model, explains how this model is an example of discursive practice, and concludes with a chapter presenting how the model relates to the career cycle of the typical teacher.

It is our hope that the ideas presented here will lead to more professionalism in the interchange among educators as we attempt to expand our skills and enable students to gain from their educational experience.

Carolyn J. Downey, San Diego State University
Betty E. Steffy, University of North Carolina at Chapel Hill
Fenwick W. English, University of North Carolina at Chapel Hill
Larry E. Frase, San Diego State University
William K. Poston, Jr., Iowa State University

Corwin Press gratefully acknowledges the contribution of the following reviewers:

Jeffrey Glanz
Author, Professor
Department of Education
Wagner College
Staten Island, NY

Karen Hayes
NSDC Board of Trustees
Assistant Professor
Department of Educational Administration and Supervision
University of Nebraska at Omaha

Mark Murphy
Nebraska AESP President
Principal
Centennial Elementary School
Utica, NE

Michael L. Friend
Executive Director
IASA
Boise, ID

Lin Kuzmich
Executive Director of Student Achievement Services
Thompson School District
Loveland, CO

Joellen Killion
Director of Special Projects
NSDC
Arvada, CO

Mark Greenberg
Assistant Principal
O'Fallon High School
O'Fallon, IL

Sue McAdamis
Coordinator of Staff Development
Rockwood School District
Eureka, MO

Edward Chevallier
Principal
Blalack Middle School
Carrollton, TX

About the Authors

Carolyn J. Downey is the creator of the walk-through process. She is currently Associate Professor of Educational Leadership in the College of Education at San Diego State University. Dr. Downey was formerly the Superintendent of Schools for the Kyrene School District, Phoenix-Tempe, Arizona. She is a nationally recognized speaker and trainer, and has assisted many of the nation's largest school systems in improving student achievement via the walk-through process. One such district is the Houston, Texas, Independent School District, which has been recognized by the Council of Great City Schools as one of the nation's four urban school systems closing the achievement gap. Dr. Downey is the originator of the *50 Ways to Close the Achievement Gap* training program and publication. She received her M.S. from the University of Southern California and her Ed.D. from Arizona State University.

Betty E. Steffy is Clinical Professor of Educational Leadership in the School of Education at the University of North Carolina at Chapel Hill. She was formerly Dean of the School of Education at Indiana University—Purdue University, Fort Wayne. She has been a professor of educational leadership at Iowa State University where she coordinated the doctoral program. She has served as the Superintendent of Schools of Moorestown, New Jersey, and was Deputy Superintendent of Instruction in the Kentucky Department of Education during the first years of the implementation of the Kentucky Education Reform Act. She is the author or coauthor of 10 books and has presented symposium papers at AERA (American Educational Research Association) and UCEA (University Council for Educational Administration). She earned her B.A., M.A.T., and Ed.D. at the University of Pittsburgh.

Fenwick W. English is the R. Wendell Eaves Distinguished Professor of Educational Leadership in the School of Education at the University of North Carolina at Chapel Hill. Dr. English is the "father" of the curriculum management audit, having directed the first such audit in Columbus, Ohio, in 1979. He also created the curriculum-mapping process in the mid-seventies. He is the author or coauthor of over 20 books and 100 journal articles. He has presented symposium papers at AERA and UCEA. He has held practitioner positions as principal, central office coordinator, assistant superintendent, and superintendent of schools. In 1988, *Executive Educator* magazine named him one of the nation's top six inservice speakers. He earned his B.S. and M.S. at the University of Southern California and his Ph.D. at Arizona State University.

Larry E. Frase is Professor and Department Chair of Educational Leadership in the College of Education at San Diego State University. He is a former superintendent of schools of the Catalina Foothills District in Tucson, Arizona, and is the author, coauthor, or editor of 23 books and 80 professional journal articles. His books include *Top Ten Myths in Education; School Management by Wandering Around;* and *Teacher Compensation and Motivation.* He is also coauthor of *Walk-Throughs and Reflective Feedback for Higher Student Achievement.* He has presented papers at AERA and UCEA. He is a senior lead auditor, having led curriculum audits of 32 school systems, including Oakland, California, and Baltimore, Maryland. Dr. Frase earned his Ed.D. at Arizona State University.

William K. Poston, Jr. is Associate Professor of Educational Leadership in the College of Education at Iowa State University, Ames, and Executive Director of the Iowa School Business Academy. Dr. Poston has written nine books and over 40 journal articles as well as presented symposium papers at UCEA. Dr. Poston is the originator of the curriculum-driven budgeting process. He served as a superintendent of schools for 15 years in Tucson and Phoenix-Tempe, Arizona, and Billings, Montana. He is past international president of Phi Delta Kappa. He has led over 60 curriculum audits in the United States and in several foreign countries including Montgomery County, Maryland; Boise, Idaho; the State of Georgia for the Georgia State Board of Education; and the government of Bermuda. He received his B.A. from the University of Northern Iowa and his Ed.D. from Arizona State University.

One's friends are that part of the human race with which one can be human.

George Santayana

All of the authors of this book dedicate it to the memory of a beloved friend and colleague, Raymond G. (Jerry) Melton. Jerry was part of our lives for four decades. We miss his infectious laugh, his support, his walk with us through the creation of so much of what has come to be called the curriculum management audit, deep alignment, and the walk-through process, the subject of this book. Like all of us, he trudged through many airports alone in all kinds of weather, but when we came together it was always the same: great warmth, cheer, jokes and, ultimately, a lighter load for all of us. We are the less for his absence and we miss him greatly. We shall not forget the good times from Tucson to Key West. Wherever you are, Jerry, we honor your friendship and remember your presence.

Understanding the Rationale Underlying the Walk-Through and Reflective Practice Approach

There are all types of classroom walk-through approaches that give feedback to teachers. Our approach is quite different from most. First, we will look at the walk-through itself. Then we will describe why a person would conduct walk-throughs of the type we propose. Finally, we will look at the development of the rationale for our approach to the five-step observation informal walk-throughs and the type of conversation we recommend to provide for optimal collaboration and reflection by teachers regarding their practice.

Before we begin this chapter, we ask you to reflect on your own experience with walk-throughs and follow-up dialogue, either as a teacher or as a supervisor/coach of teachers. You may do this alone, or if you are working with a learning partner, you might enjoy doing this together. The following questions might start you on your reflective thoughts:

- How often do you or did your supervisor walk into the classroom?
- How long do you or did your supervisor stay in the classroom on these walk-throughs?
- How frequently do you or did your supervisor provide follow-up?
- What was the nature of the follow-up?

REFLECTION

Initial Reflections on Walk-Throughs and Follow-Up

(Write your comments here.)

_____

_____

_____

_____

WHAT IS THE DOWNEY WALK-THROUGH?

Downey Walk-Throughs involve five key ideas:

1. Short, focused, yet informal observation. The Downey Walk-Through classroom visit is short in length—about 2 to 3 minutes in a classroom. It is like taking a short video clip of the moment. There is no intent to evaluate the teacher; rather it is a time to gather information about curricular and instructional teaching practices and decisions teachers are making. It has been said that a teacher makes over 1,000 decisions a day. Our experience is that in the 2 to 3 minutes we are in the classroom, we typically observe anywhere from 5 to 10 decisions being made.

To focus our time in the classroom, the walk-through includes a five-step observational structure for gathering information on both the curriculum being taught and the instructional teaching decisions being made. This is described in detail in Chapter 2.

If you have about 30 minutes to walk through some classrooms, you could visit 10 to 12 classrooms using our approach. With other walk-through approaches, the observer usually stays in the room from 10 to 15 minutes. This would allow for only 2 or 3 classroom visits in 30 minutes. Through frequent, short observations, you become familiar with the teaching patterns and decisions teachers are making on a daily basis. Over time, you will obtain far more information about teachers and the school when you stay in each classroom for just a few minutes per visit.

Occasionally, you might spend more time in a classroom, but this is not the norm for our walk-through approach. If our goal is one of professional growth rather than evaluation of the individual, a short visit is all that is required to provide ample data to promote teacher growth. With a longer stay, too much data are collected. In fact, it is our opinion that we tend to make more judgments when staying in classrooms for longer periods of time. The short observation allows you to frequent all the classrooms on a regular basis rather than see just a few a month. The principal will have a more accurate picture of what is going on in the school when he or she is able to visit all of the classrooms regularly.

2. Possible area for reflection. The major goal of this brief informal observation is to trigger a thought that might be useful for the teacher to consider, one that might help the teacher in his or her decision making about effective practice. Notice the language here—"might be useful." When we provide follow-up, it is to give opportunities for reflective thought. The *teachers* will decide whether our conversation is of value to them. There are times for direct feedback, and this will be discussed later; but the ultimate purpose of our walk-through with reflective dialogue is to enable every educator to become a reflective thinker. Reflective thinkers are people who are personally responsible for their own growth and who are continuously analyzing their practice. An entire chapter (Chapter 3) is devoted to the reflective conversation.

3. Curriculum as well as instructional focus. While you are in the classroom observing, you will want to gather data about the curriculum and instructional decisions being made and notice their impact on student behavior. You will want to focus on curriculum and pedagogy. Typically, you will not be in the classroom long enough to ascertain content accuracy and completeness. We will share the strategy for moving out of the classroom after you have had a chance to zero in on the teaching objective and think of an effective teaching practice that you might want to discuss with the teacher (see Chapter 2).

4. Follow-up occurs only on occasion and not after every visit. While you are in the classroom, think about whether you wish to have a conversation with the teacher about any decisions the teacher is making. This needs to be done before you move to the next classroom. Decide whether you will be providing a follow-up conversation on some teaching practice for reflection (see Chapter 3). We would suggest that follow-up conversations not take place every time you visit a classroom. You may want to visit a classroom as many as 8 to 10 times before you decide to engage the teacher in reflective dialogue. In fact, we would suggest that feedback be given only when you know it will be received in a meaningful and timely manner. We will talk about various follow-up approaches and ways to keep them brief in Chapter 3.

5. *Informal and collaborative.* There is no checklist of things to look for or judgments to be made. Checklists signal a formal observation and one that often looks like an inspection to the teacher. Our approach is informal, informal, and informal! With this process you do not go into a classroom with a checklist of teacher skills you wish to see, nor do you make a duplicate copy of your notes that is given to the teacher and/or placed in a file.

Our approach is very different. It is about colleagues working together to help each other think about practice. It is not about judging a teacher's effective use of a given teaching practice. While you are in the classroom, you will need to do an analysis and may need to take a few notes, but these notes are only to remind you of something you might want to remember. You will be going into so many classrooms; the notes will be necessary to jog your memory. We will make suggestions on how to take these notes and also on how to let teachers know what you are recording and why.

Table 1.1 lists some key ideas about our approach to walk-throughs compared to approaches used by other educators.

Table 1.1   Comparison of Walk-Through Approaches

Our Approach	*Other Approaches*
Informal	Formal
Brief—2 to 3 minutes	Longer—5 to 15 minutes
Brief gathering of data to look for teacher decisions	Gather data about teacher effectiveness
Walk-through time is throughout the day and unannounced	Walk-through time is typically known and scheduled—to watch a teacher use "shared reading strategies," for example
No checklist of teaching practices to look for; focus on curricular and instructional decision points of the teacher	Specific checklist (rubric) type of form to gather data about specific practices
Nothing put into personnel file	May be put into personnel file
Focus on professional growth	Focus on evaluation, assessment
Ultimately leads to reflective conversation	Usually leads to direct feedback from the supervisor to the teacher
Coaching focus	Judging focus—often inspectional

It should be mentioned that there are times when you are going to make more formal walk-through observations. You might want to spend more time with novice teachers and look for certain skills, such as classroom management proficiencies. If you think you have a marginal teacher, you will want to stay longer and make judgments that are documented. You might want to conduct classroom data-gathering observations on particular practices to help determine group staff-development needs. But remember, these formal walk-throughs should be fairly infrequent and out of the norm. Also, teachers must be made aware of exactly why you are going to do a formal walk-through.

This book is written for the majority of teachers, who are in good standing and trying to impact student achievement in the classroom.

Please take a moment to think about what you have read so far regarding our approach and about your previous experience with walk-throughs and follow-up dialogue. Think about similarities and differences between our approach and your previous experiences. Write your ideas below, on your own or together with your learning partner.

REFLECTION

What Are Your Reflections About Our Approach in Relation to Your Experiences Regarding Walk-Throughs and Follow-Up Dialogue?

(Write your comments here.)

_____

_____

_____

_____

WHY WALK-THROUGHS?

Think for a moment about why you would conduct brief walk-throughs in classrooms. Why do you think walk-throughs are of value? Why should walk-throughs be a high priority in your work?

REFLECTION

Why Should Walk-Throughs Be a High Priority in Your Work?

(Write your comments here.)

_____

_____

_____

_____

Here are some of our reasons for brief walk-throughs (Downey & Frase, 2001). Notice how many of your reasons are the same as ours.

- The frequent sampling of a teacher's actions gives greater validity to what you observe.
- Frequent observations often lower teacher apprehension over time, making formal observations more effective.
- The more you know about how people are functioning and making decisions, the more you know about the school's operations.
- The more you observe, the more you learn—the greater the repertoire of strategies you can share with other staff.
- You can identify common areas of decisions that might prove valuable for group staff development—entire faculty, department level, and grade level groups.
- You can observe how effective your staff development endeavors have been in impacting teaching behavior in the classroom.
- If parents call about a concern, you have your own observational data, in most cases, of the teacher's intentions and practice. You are better informed.
- It helps you identify possible individuals who might become marginal if you do not provide assistance quickly.
- It helps you keep perspective about your work.

What else did you think about that has not been mentioned? What has been mentioned here that you would add to your list? Add to your list below:

REFLECTION

Add to Your List of Reasons for Walk-Throughs

(Write your comments here.)

_____

_____

_____

_____

It is essential that you take the time to interact with staff about their practices. Our walk-through approach is a valuable vehicle to start this journey toward collaborative, reflective dialogue. The teacher must be the primary client of the school-based administrator, whereas the district's primary client and the teacher's primary client is the student. The only way you are going to effect higher student achievement is through the teacher and his or her actions in the classroom.

Richard Elmore (2000) points out that administrators spend a great deal of time making changes in the structure of the organization. However, most of these changes do not result in higher student achievement. He indicates that it is not until we are impacting what is happening in the classroom that we will see higher student achievement.

Obviously, the principal has clients other than teachers, such as the parents and students. But often the principal views him- or herself as being most responsible to students and being less so to teachers. Other principals view their primary role as one of only maintaining a smooth-running organization. It is time for this minimalist image to change, but in order for that to happen, principals and other administrators must come to view their primary role as one of an instructional leader promoting improved student achievement. This requires that principals spend a lot of time visiting classrooms and engaging teachers in collaborative, reflective dialogue.

Gene Hall and Shirley Hord (2000), who have studied the principal's role for years, have found that brief, one-on-one, focused feedback (one-legged conversation) is the most powerful staff development approach available to impact and change behavior. It is certainly more powerful than the typical one-day workshop many teachers attend. Our approach is to have 3- to 5-minute conversations with teachers that lead them into future thought.

We have three ultimate goals for the walk-through approach with collaborative, reflective dialogue. They are listed in Table 1.2.

Table 1.2   Ultimate Goals of the Walk-Through Approach With Reflective Dialogue*

- Reflective, self-directed, self-analytical, interdependent teachers who examine their own practices (even those who initially are at the dependent level)
- Teachers who are continually willing to improve their teaching practices
- Teachers who are committed to teaching the district curriculum student learnings and to working for ever higher student achievement

* The term *teacher* could be replaced with any type of educational position.

As we describe our approach in more detail in the following chapters, you will come to see how we use these strategies to achieve these goals.

People who hear about our approach to collaborative, reflective dialogue are intrigued, as it is very different from the approach most people use or have experienced. We consider it a 21st-century technique that honors teachers and their work and that focuses on those things that influence higher student achievement.

As mentioned earlier in this book, the approach being described was developed by Dr. Carolyn Downey, and it has evolved over time. Dr. Downey has served as an administrator in various roles for over 30 years. Among its most important attributes and key ideas, Downey's approach

- Focuses on those factors that influence higher student achievement
- Assumes there is alignment among the written, taught, and assessed curriculum
- Encourages teachers to provide instruction at the right level of difficulty for each student
- Promotes teacher use of assessments for diagnostic purposes to determine prerequisites, and acquisition and mastery of the learning

The collaborative, reflective dialogue following classroom visits

- Builds on the fact that change is intrapersonal—it comes from within
- Focuses on the use of intrinsic motivational strategies that honor the teacher and his or her decisions versus telling the teacher what to do
- Recognizes the teacher's level of experience and readiness for self-direction
- Engages in dialogue that moves the teacher to self-analysis
- Encourages collegial interactions and enables educators to learn together in an interdependent way

Our approach is very powerful with respect to change and the working relationship between coach/supervisor and teacher. We are not into a "gotcha" approach. Our goal is not to embarrass or put any teacher into a defensive posture. Rather, our goal is to have collaborative, thoughtful interactions with our colleagues. However, should our approach not be used in the way it was designed, it could be turned into a "gotcha" approach.

For those in supervisory roles with teachers, the shift should be away from a conventional or congenial supervisory approach toward a collegial one. Glickman, Gordon, and Ross-Gordon (1998) describe this shift as follows, that the relationship needs to be

- Collegial rather than a hierarchical relationship between teachers and supervisors
- Focused on teacher development rather than teacher conformity
- Facilitative of teachers collaborating with each other in instructional improvement efforts
- Supportive of teacher involvement in ongoing reflective inquiry

THE EVOLUTION OF THE DOWNEY WALK-THROUGH PROCESS

This particular walk-though approach began in the 1960s. Downey tells the story of becoming an administrator in the mid-60s and how someone indicated she ought to get into classrooms. Thinking it was a good idea, she proceeded to do so merely from a symbolic perspective—to let staff know she cared about them and their work. Staff responded well to these short visits. Downey quickly began to realize, however, that there was much more to the walk-throughs than just the symbolism of her presence. She began to get a big picture of the learning environment and saw how much one could learn from the walk-throughs. She realized that there were many strategies and techniques that she had never used as a teacher that could become part of her staff's repertoire—strategies that she could share with others and use for staff development (Downey & Frase, 2001).

Over the years, Downey came to realize that the walk-through, coupled with meaningful dialogue, was a most effective approach to focus on staff members' professional growth. In the late 1960s, Downey had the opportunity to learn the Madeline Hunter (1968) approach to teacher evaluation. In this process, the administrator was supposed to intervene in the teacher's practice by suggesting strategies for improvement and behaviors to be maintained. She began to use these same strategies for walk-through conversation.

In the early 1970s, Downey went to a training with Sue Wells Welsh (1971), who added a self-analysis portion to the Hunter model. Downey indicates that this is when the journey toward reflective thought began for her. It was not only in her formal evaluations of staff that she focused on self-analysis; in the follow-up after walk-throughs, she began to move away from complimentary closing comments and began to use conversation with self-reflection. Downey indicates that this was philosophically more in line with her thinking about how to motivate staff toward change. Rather than telling or selling an idea, individuals exposed to new ideas seemed to embrace them better through reflective dialogue than when the "boss" told them how to change or reinforce certain practices.

In the early 1970s, through Costa's (1994; Costa & Garmston, 1985) training on Cognitive Coaching, Downey's approach to the reflective model was enhanced. Although the training was about the formal evaluation process, Downey began to move more and more toward the informal, brief walk-through with a focus on reflective conversations with teachers.

As Downey states, "The idea of moving from an inspectional approach to supervision to a reflectional supervision approach began to take shape. Why would anyone want to be in an inspectional situation unless the person was seen as marginal?" Where the Hunter model involved direct intervention, the Costa model was teacher-led and involved self-reflection on a topic selected by the teacher. Downey found herself caught between these two models and began to create one of her own. Her model was moving toward a more collaborative and interdependent practice in which reflection was the focus. She found that the Hunter approach was working quite well with relatively inexperienced teachers and marginal teachers and that the Costa model, as it was described in the early 1970s, was working for the teachers who were experienced and especially for those who were quite independent.

During this time, Downey was influenced further by two different ideas about supervision that added to her perspective concerning identification of a continuum of reflective interaction. This evolved into the identification of three types of reflective dialogue that are incorporated into the model today: direct, indirect, and collaborative, reflective dialogue. One influence was Stephen Covey (1989), who advocated moving employees from a dependent relationship with a supervisor to an interdependent relationship, going through the independent stage along the way. This provided Downey with the logic for differentiation because it moved from the indirect or independent relationship with a supervisor to one that could be collaborative.

A second influence for Downey was Eric Berne's transactional analysis (1963), which described the supervisor's relationship with employees as adult-child, adult-adolescent, and adult-adult. Downey combined Covey and Berne in her thinking. She did not embrace the ideas of Berne or Covey in total but felt the information was of value when assessing the supervisory process.

As depicted in Figure 1.1, the dependent relationship is one of adult-child. This often benefits the novice teacher who needs a supportive, nurturing relationship that is direct in nature and in which the supervisor is in a teaching role. However, it is important that we move from that dependency stage to one of interdependence. Many supervisors use the same dependency style with experienced teachers, which has a very different effect on the teacher. Many experienced staff members actually enjoy this relationship—a paternalistic, benevolent one. The independent level was described as the

Figure 1.1   Flow of Supervisor of/Employee Relationships

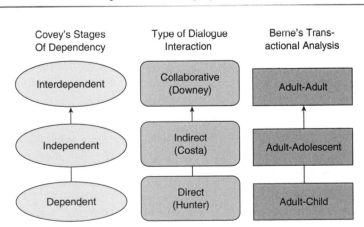

adult-adolescent relationship between supervisor and employee. The ideal was noted as the interdependent, collaborative, adult-adult relationship. We want to have professional conversations with our teachers that are collaborative—adults to adults, learning together.

By the 1980s, Downey's model had continued to evolve in several ways:

- The supervisor acted as coach and mentor rather than judge.
- The supervisor viewed the teacher as the primary client for impacting student achievement.
- Interaction between principal and teacher moved from extrinsic motivators such as notes and positive praise to intrinsic motivations focused on teacher efficacy.
- Occasion for providing follow-up moved from giving feedback after every visit toward an occasional, collaborative, reflective dialogue, typically in the form of a reflective question.
- Conversations with novice/apprentice teachers who needed direct, nurturing feedback took on a reflective component.
- Supervisors began to recognize that it is the teacher's choice to answer any substantial reflective question posed by the supervisor, and that the teacher should be given time to ponder such questions.
- The focus moved toward encouraging reflective inquiry by teachers on their practices and decisions and moved away from direct feedback from a supervisor.
- It was recognized that it is the reflective question that has the power to change what teachers believe.
- There was a strengthening of the belief that the ultimate goal of supervision is to facilitate each teacher's ability to be self-analyzing about practice.

A few more ideas should be mentioned about how Downey views supervision. When she first began to focus on what was happening in the classroom, her observations were centered on instructional teaching practices, since most of her training had been in this area. In the 1980s, Downey was influenced by Fenwick English (1988) and his work on the alignment of the written, taught, and assessed curriculum (1993). Downey began to focus not only on how teachers were teaching but also on what they were teaching. This curriculum and instructional focus became entrenched in her model and has now been in place for over a decade and a half.

The more recent stage in the evolution of the Downey Walk-Through is *the focus on teacher decisions rather than on teacher actions*. There is more

Figure 1.2   Professional Growth Cycle

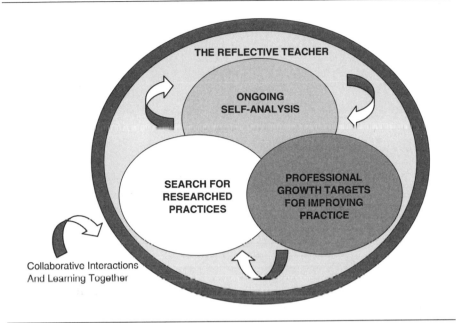

focus on reflection about how teachers will make instructional decisions in the future. Observing teacher decisions enables the teacher and principal to open up a dialogue about the criteria being used in the making of those decisions.

As Downey began teaching others her approach, she refined the components of the reflective question and conversation. This approach will be described in detail in Chapter 3.

The brief yet focused walk-through followed by collaborative, reflective dialogue is very powerful in bringing about change. Its ultimate purpose is to support teachers in becoming responsible and self-analytical individuals who are continuously improving their practice. After this goal is reached, teachers are encouraged to set growth targets and to search out researched practices and try them. Thus the cycle of self-analysis and improvement continues. This cycle of renewal is illustrated in Figure 1.2.

The heading of this figure could have been "The Reflective Principal," "The Reflective Superintendent," or "The Reflective Secretary"—the idea is for *every* employee to be continually growing.

Downey states that when she began supervising staff, she believed that she could go directly from her thoughts to her actions to change teacher behavior. Then she realized that this is not the way to implement truly long-lasting change. What she should be doing with her thoughts is influencing the thoughts of the teacher. This approach continues as it is

Figure 1.3   Initial Purpose of Follow-Up Interaction (influenced by Costa)

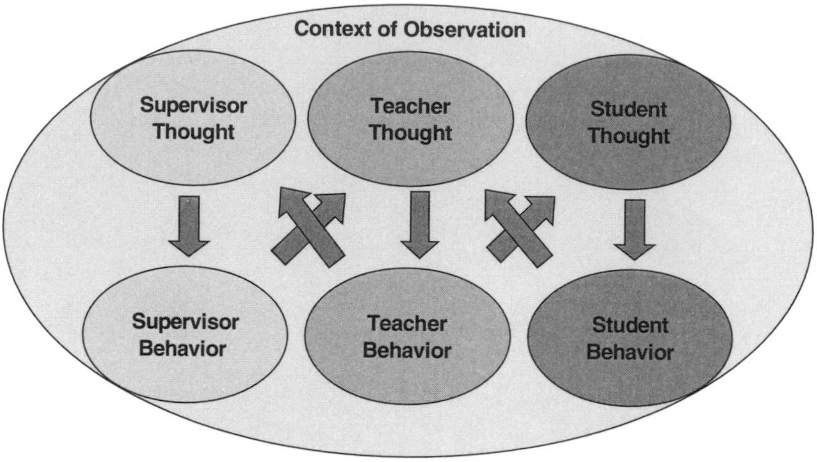

then used by the teacher as he or she works with students. It is also fully reciprocal in that the goal of the teacher would then be to influence the thoughts of the coach and/or supervisor. This is illustrated in Figure 1.3.

As noted:

- Our goal as supervisors is not to change teacher behavior but rather to influence a teacher's thinking so that the teacher has a desire to change his or her own behavior.
- Then the teacher's thinking will influence the teacher's behavior, which in turn influences student thought to obtain the desired student behaviors.
- And finally, the teacher's thinking influences the teacher's behavior to consequently influence supervisory thinking.
- This is a reciprocal process of influencing one another's reflective inquiries into one's own practice and work.

Table 1.3 provides a summary of the key ideas embodied in our approach to walk-through follow-up conversations versus some of the other walk-through models being used today.

Table 1.3   Comparison of Follow-Up Approaches

Our Approach	*Other Approaches*
Focus on moving all staff to self-reflection, self-diagnosis, and continual professional growth.	Focus on ensuring a particular instructional practice is in place in a classroom

Our Approach	*Other Approaches*
Two-way and conversational, with reflection (different levels); little, if any, use of notes	Direct feedback—often use of one-way notes or a checklist
Recognizes different levels of follow-up—direct, indirect, interactive	Follow-up is mainly direct feedback
Focus is on reflective questions about one's practice—not about the lesson observed	Focus is usually on the lesson observed and a particular practice and on how to improve that practice
Reflectional supervision philosophy with focus on teacher reflection at the analysis, synthesis, or evaluation cognitive type	More of an inspectional philosophy of accountability for particular practices—expected compliance
Focus on cycle of professional renewal	Focus on today's practice
Focus on intrinsic motivation	Focus on extrinsic motivation

It's Your Reflection Time!

Think back to the start of this chapter and your thoughts about walk-throughs and follow-up. How has this chapter influenced your thoughts?

Current Reflections About the Downey
Walk-Through and Follow-Up Approach

(Write your comments here.)

_____

_____

_____

_____

Conducting the Walk-Through Observation

A Five-Step Process

We now present the five-step process in detail. When these steps are in place, they provide a focus for the observer. The structure allows an individual to be in the classroom for a short period of time and gain much information that may be used later to facilitate teachers' reflections about their decisions. Multiple observations of the same teacher over time enhance the power of the observations to provide the maximum information in the compressed time capsules available to busy school administrators and supervisors during any given week in the school year.

Before the five steps are presented, take a moment to think about what you do when you conduct walk-throughs in classrooms. Then you will be able to compare what you do with what we do. These questions might start you on your reflective thoughts:

- What do you pay attention to first?
- What do you do, for example, walk around, look at student work, talk with students, talk to the teacher?
- What do you observe?
- What do you do with the data you gather?

REFLECTION

My Walk-Throughs

(Write your comments here.)

_____

_____

_____

_____

Read through the walk-through outline of a classroom visit that follows. We have chosen to introduce the model in this way because it provides you with a specific example of what you might see in a classroom. If you have gone through the Downey Walk-Through training, you will recognize that this format is similar to how we introduce the model utilizing videotapes of classroom teaching. If you have a videotape of a teaching episode, you may want to use it for this exercise. The scenarios in this chapter show you the kind of notations we would make and how we would use what we learned during the classroom observation to engage the teacher in a reflective conversation. (Note: While we make suggestions about reflective dialogue based on the scenarios included here, in reality you would not want to engage a teacher in reflective dialogue based on only a single visit to the classroom.)

The following classroom scenario is set in a 12th-grade language arts class. This actual observation took 3 minutes.

Scenario One: 12th-Grade Language Arts

[Students all looking at the teacher. Teacher at the board. On the board the words *iambic* and *anapestic*. Teacher is pointing to the word *iambic*.]

Teacher: How many syllables does it need to have?

Choral response: Six. [About half the students.]

Teacher:	And you have to say this in your head: Iambic pentameter. One of the things we mix this up with is "anapestic." I need someone to come to the board and write three anapestic feet. [Five students raise their hands.] Virginia.
Virginia:	[Student goes to the board and illustrates symbolically three anapestic feet and then walks back to her desk.]
Teacher:	Thank you. What is the critical difference between an iambic and anapestic foot? [A few students raise their hands.] If you know, raise your hand with an open hand. If you know but don't want to be called on, raise your hand with a closed hand. If you don't know, raise your hand and cup your hand [to tell me] "I don't know what the difference is and I am confused." [All students raise their hands, most with an open hand.] John.
John:	Anapestic has three and iambic has two.
Teacher:	Yes, not words but . . .
Choral student response:	Syllables. [Almost all students.]
Teacher:	That's right. Not words but syllables. And, that is confusing. What is the next critical thing? [Eight students raise their hands.] Susan.
Susan:	Anapestic has two unstressed.
Teacher:	Two unstressed and one . . .?
Choral student response:	Stressed. [Almost all students.]
Teacher:	How many total syllables?
Choral student response:	Nine. [Almost all students.]
Teacher:	This was so easy on the board. When we clap it seems easy, too; but when we write it, it is harder. Let's practice this clapping. Clap on 3, three anapestic feet. 1, 2, 3.
Student clapping:	[All students clapping, about two or three students clapping incorrectly.]

Teacher:	Good. Clap on 3, two iambic and three anapestic feet. 1, 2, 3.
Student clapping:	[All students clapping, about three or four students clapping incorrectly.]
Teacher:	Clap on 3, one anapestic, one iambic, one anapestic, one iambic. [Small groan from class with smiles.] 1, 2, 3.
Student clapping:	[All students clapping, about six students clapping incorrectly.]
Teacher:	Very good. I know those of you who didn't quite get it will practice it. Let's now look at some literature and see if we can distinguish between the two types of sonnets.

Using the space provided, write down what you observed and what follow-up comments you might give to the teacher, if desired.

> **My Observations and Possible Follow-Up Areas for the Language Arts Classroom**
>
> (Write your comments here.)
>
> _____
>
> _____
>
> _____
>
> _____

THE FIVE-STEP OBSERVATION STRUCTURE

The goal of our walk-through approach is to gather focused data in a very short period of time. During most observations we have one area that we wish to see—students oriented to the work. Other than that, and very important, we look for both the curricular and instructional

Table 2.1   Quick Overview of the Five-Step Walk-Through Observation
Structure

Step 1: Student Orientation to the Work—Do students appear to be
attending when you first walk into the room?

Step 2: Curricular Decision Points—What objective(s) has the teacher
chosen to teach at this time and how aligned are they to the
prescribed (district or state) written curriculum?

Step 3: Instructional Decision Points—What instructional practices is
the teacher choosing to use at this time to help students achieve the
learning of the curriculum objectives?

Step 4: "Walk-the-Walls": Curricular and Instructional Decisions—
What evidence is there of past objectives taught and/or instructional
decisions used to teach the objectives that are present in the
classroom—walk-the-walls, portfolios, projects in the room?

Step 5: Safety and Health Issues—Are there any noticeable safety or
health issues that need to be addressed?

decisions the teacher is choosing to make. We make no judgment about
the teacher's practices. Table 2.1 is a quick preview of our five steps.
Always do the first three steps and pick up Steps 4 and 5 based on time
and observation.

Each step of the five-step process is described in detail below and is
used to analyze the same scenario you just observed.

STEP 1: STUDENT ORIENTATION TO WORK

The first step is completed within the first two seconds (hopefully before
we are noticed by the students). The goal of this step is to notice whether
students appear to be oriented to the work. The work could be listening and
interacting with the teacher, with other students, or working alone. We
are not concerned with the nature of the student work or what the
teacher is doing to keep students engaged. This is just a quick look to
see if attending behavior seems to be in place. Attending behavior is a
prerequisite to learning.

We do not count the number of students engaged. This step is just a *cursory glance.* If, however, we see nonattending behavior on numerous visits,
we need to be observant as to what might be creating the off-task behavior.

The best time to gather this information is before the students see you.
If there are windows in the room, you might gather this information
before entering. If the door is open or opens without squeaking, you may

be able to quickly ascertain attending behavior. If the door squeaks and students notice you, try not to make eye contact with students or engage the students so that the teacher may continue business as usual. If you cause a distraction but the students go back to task quickly or the teacher brings their focus back to the work, this is fine. You want to be as unobtrusive as possible in Step 1 of your observation.

Blase and Blase (1998) indicate that teachers like to have administrators in their rooms, but not when they distract students from their work. *Be careful that you do not take students off task.* At times you may desire to engage in conversation with students, but make sure that it is not simply to meet your observational needs. When you walk into the room, remember that your primary client is the teacher. You must try not be distracted by student behavior; students are experts at knowing how to engage visitors so that they do not have to do their work.

Often the physical setup of the room will cause you to be a distraction. If the door places you at the front of the room, quickly walk to the back of the room. Another distraction may occur if the teacher stops to talk with you. You must clarify for teachers that they are to ignore you and carry on with their work whenever you walk into the room, unless you specifically ask for their attention. Many teachers believe that administrators are to be acknowledged and honored when they come into the room. You probably will have to talk one-on-one with these teachers to help them refrain from this practice. You cannot observe teachers who are engaged with the observers.

Frequently the teacher will begin to explain what the students are learning or have a student come and share what the students are learning. This would be informative for visitors, but you are not a visitor. You are part of the learning environment. Because some habits are hard to break, be persistent with teachers on this point.

Downey relates the story of walking around a high school with a principal: In every classroom entered, the teacher stopped what he or she was doing and informed them of what the students were learning at that moment. After about a dozen classrooms, Downey asked the principal about this behavior. The principal explained that it was the teachers' practice and stated that she had, on several occasions, asked the teachers to not do this. When questioned further about why she thought they were continuing to stop teaching when the principal entered their rooms, she indicated that it was mainly so they would not be observed. Downey pressed the principal on this point, asking if it just might be a habit. The principal said she did not think so, because she had tried so hard to implement this change. They went on to discuss strategies to help teachers be comfortable with the principal coming into the classrooms to observe.

Step 1 should be very brief, and its only purpose is to notice if students are instructionally oriented. However, we cannot really know if they are paying attention. This is why we do not use it to assess an "engagement rate." At times students appear to be paying attention but really are not. This becomes evident if a student is asked a question about the content and cannot respond, or if asked to follow along when the teacher is reading and he or she is on the wrong page. We are not concerned with these instances since our interest is in getting a cursory measure of the degree of orientation of the students to the work. This is mainly a classroom management issue. If there is frequent off-task behavior by many students, direct action should be taken to assist the teacher in developing classroom management skills.

Analysis of the Language Arts Scenario for Step 1:

The box below includes the information you might have recorded for Step 1.

Box 2.1   Language Arts Scenario—Step 1: Student Orientation to the Work

Fine. Students oriented to teacher.

STEP 2: CURRICULAR DECISION POINTS

After the very quick Step 1, we spend the majority of the two to three minutes in the classroom delineating the actual curricular objective(s) we see being taught. We want to determine the content of the student learning.

Content is the skill, knowledge, process, or concept to be learned by the students. Identifying the curricular objective is the first part of Step 2. Most of us tend to focus immediately on the instructional practices in our observations rather than on the curriculum standards and objectives being taught. We become absorbed in the instructional decisions a teacher is making and miss the curricular objectives being taught.

The basic purpose of Step 2 is to determine the alignment of the taught curriculum with the written or prescribed curriculum (English, 1993). In order to make a determination, we must derive the curriculum content and then ascertain where the objective falls in the district (or state) curriculum.

Table 2.2   Example of Scope and Sequence Chart for Calibration Purposes

Kindergarten Number Sense	Grade One Number Sense	Grade Two Number Sense
K.1 Count, recognize, represent, name, and order a number of objects (up to 30).	1.1 Count, read, and write whole numbers to 100.	2.1 Count, read, and write whole numbers to 1,000 and identify the place value for each digit.
K.2 Compare two or more sets of objects (up to 10 objects in each group) and identify which set is equal to, more than, or less than the other.	1.2 Compare and order whole numbers to 100 by using the symbols for less than, equal to, or greater than $(<, =, >)$.	2.2 Use words, models, and expanded forms (e.g., $45 = 4$ tens $+ 5$) to represent numbers (up to 1,000).
		2.3 Order and compare whole numbers to 1,000 by using the symbols $<, =, >$.

At some point, either while in the classroom or after returning to the office or other place where the curriculum can be accessed online, we examine curriculum documents to determine whether and where the objectives are located in the prescribed, written curriculum. Many districts develop a scope and sequence of the content across grades and courses for their school-based administrators and teacher coaches. The hard copy of this document is organized to be easily read, light in weight, and laminated for carrying purposes. Some principals have downloaded the scope and sequence charts into their electronic organizers. An example of how this might look can be found above in Table 2.2.

To calibrate the lessons, locate the objective being taught in the district's (or state's) prescribed, written curriculum. Downey has worked with several districts to set up an easy way to review the curriculum objectives on the spot. Objectives listed in table format by course or grade are very helpful tools for review, especially if they are computerized.

It is important that your calibration be descriptive only. You should not speculate as to why the teacher has chosen one objective over another. Even though we may find the objective to be below or above the grade observed, the teacher may have good reason for this.

Data from thousands of observations made over the past few years portray a discouraging general trend. The more a student moves up the grade levels, the less likely it is that the observed objective will be on grade level. Rather, it will typically be below grade level. This trend is found in schools serving children from all socioeconomic levels, and it definitely holds true in those schools identified as low performing.

Another interesting but perplexing and disturbing observation made over the years is that even district-adopted textbooks use objectives that are below grade level. And most teachers let the textbooks rather than the written curriculum direct what they are teaching. This certainly is an area in which staff development is needed across the nation.

What should be done when you find a teacher teaching below grade level? Do you judge this as wrong? Absolutely not—this is not about judgment. There are many instructional reasons why a teacher might choose to be teaching a particular objective. The calibration simply allows administrators to see patterns in the teachers' curricular decisions. It also may begin to throw light on the instructional decisions a teacher might be making. For example, you may have walked in when the teacher was reviewing or bringing forward prior learning to aid in teaching a new concept. Or, it could be that through diagnostic assessments the teacher had determined that the students did not have the prerequisite knowledge for the desired on-grade level or course level learning outcomes. All of this information helps principals when they confer with staff about their curricular and instructional decisions. It also provides the principal with data for potential reflective questions, which are described in detail in Chapter 3.

What happens if you find several objectives being worked on at the same time when you walk into a classroom? Don't try to note all of them. If you do, you might find yourself in the room for 15 minutes. Observe the teacher and note only the objective with which the teacher is directly involved. It might be whole-group work, small-group work, or the teacher working one-on-one with a student. If there is another teacher or aide in the classroom, also determine the objective that adult is working with before you leave. *Try to identify no more than two or three objectives when multiple activities are being conducted.* At times a student might be working with many different worksheets. Just pick the specific objective on which the student is currently working, then move to another student until you pick up another objective, and then move out of the room.

Typically, you will not get an accurate reading of the objective by standing at the back of the room. Being as unobtrusive as possible, you must view the actual work that students are doing. Go beyond reading the heading of a worksheet. It might not correctly reflect or represent the objective or give you all the information you need.

Try not to talk with students if it takes them off task. However, if you think that asking a few students what they are learning will help determine the objective, without being too disruptive, you might talk with a student for just a few seconds. Ask the question, "What are you learning?" not "What are you doing?" With the latter, students will typically describe the activity rather than the learning. Repeat the question to determine the objective and make sure to ask more than one student—you might find different answers.

Analysis of the Language Arts Scenario for Step 2

The box below includes information you might have recorded for the first part of Step 2.

Box 2.2   Language Arts Scenario—Step 2: Curriculum Decision Points

---

Content Taught: Distinguish between an iambic and anapestic foot (syllables and stress) that might be used in a sonnet.

Course: 12th-grade English

District Calibration: Could be a prerequisite objective in the district's 7th-grade English curriculum course [from a real district's curriculum scope and sequence: "Use iambic and anapestic feet in writing a sonnet."].

One might ask why a 12th-grade teacher would be teaching a 7th-grade objective. It could be that it was a prerequisite to a new learning. Or it could be that the objective is on a high-stakes test and the students did not do well on this topic. Later we will ask a reflective question (see Chapter 3) that enables the teacher to reflect on the criteria that should be used to select the objectives to be taught. Again, the purpose of Step 2 is only to gather the data.

Once you are comfortable identifying the content of the objective(s) being taught, you can begin to examine more detailed information about the objective—what Downey and Frase (2001) call *the 3 C's—Content, Context, and Cognitive type.* Table 2.3 outlines the 3 C's:

The first "C" is "Content" (the objective). The second "C" is "Context." The context of an objective is very important for what is called "deep alignment" (English & Steffy, 2001). Context, how teachers have students

Table 2.3   Analysis of the Student Objective(s)—The 3 C's

Content: The skill, knowledge, process, concept to be learned by the students

Context: The conditions under which students will demonstrate the learning (e.g., student mode of response, materials and information given to them orally or in writing)

Cognitive Type: Knowledge, comprehension, application, analysis, synthesis, evaluation (Bloom et al., 1956)

practice the content of the objective, is essential for helping students transfer the learnings outside of the classroom situation. One critical place we want students to transfer their learning is to external, high-stakes assessments. But, perhaps the most important transfer is to "real-world" situations.

Crucial to the concept of deep alignment is the work of Thorndike (1913, 1951). Thorndike found that transfer of learnings to new situations was easier when the situational contexts were similar. But how do we make the instructional context of classrooms similar to the context where the student must demonstrate what he or she knows on a state accountability assessment? This is accomplished by on some occasions making the pedagogy in the classroom similar to the test format. This is a very simple suggestion but one that is seldom practiced consistently in classrooms.

English and Steffy (2001) discuss topological alignment and deep alignment. They define these terms as follows:

- *Topological Alignment*—A generic "match" between the test curriculum content and classroom content and context aligned with some sequencing considerations
- *Deep Alignment*—Creation of maximum pedagogical and environmental congruence between the teaching and the testing situations in both content and context using many alternative forms of assessment

Typically, the context of an objective involves questions that are oral in nature or, if written, that require short, fill-in answers. The transferability of these responses to other contexts is weak. Teachers need to practice and test students in multiple contexts to aid in their transfer of the learning.

There are at least three elements involved in the context of an objective:

- *Givens*—Material that is given to the student in the form of directions (oral or in writing), and other information such as graphs or a word problem.
- *Nature of the Student Response*—How is the student to respond? By writing, speaking, pointing, circling, or bubbling in?
- *Special Vocabulary*—Any vocabulary that is essential to understanding the particular content of the objective.

The third "C" is the "Cognitive type," from Bloom, Englehard, Furst, Hill, and Krathwohl's (1956) *Taxonomy of Educational Objectives: Cognitive Domain.* It is important to note that in the research conducted by Bloom and others, the levels are not considered hierarchical (see Cezak, Webb, & Kalohn, 1995), but they are useful in our application to describe the desired type of thinking.

Analysis of the Language Arts Scenario That Is Part of Step 2

Box 2.3   Language Arts Scenario—Step 2: Curriculum Decision Points

---

Content Taught: Distinguish between an iambic and anapestic foot (syllables and stress) that might be used in a sonnet.

Context of the Taught Content:

- Given—oral directions to describe differences or to clap
- Nature of the student response—oral, hand clapping
- Special vocabulary—iambic, anapestic, sonnet

Cognitive Type: Knowledge

If the information recorded so far was reflective of a trend or pattern based on a number of classroom visits, it could lead to a reflective dialogue with the teacher around a number of topics such as the selection of what is given to the student, the nature of the student response, as well as the thinking approach desired.

Table 2.4   Florida Sunshine Example

Think, Solve, and Explain
(Florida "Performance Tasks" Short Answer)

Draw a circle around each quadrilateral shown below

On the lines below, explain why all the shapes you circled are quadrilaterals.

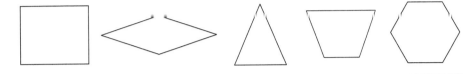

To further elaborate on the value of noting and reflecting on the context of an objective, we will take a sample item from the Florida practice tests and deconstruct it for content and context.

Read the sample test item in Table 2.4, complete it, and then identify the content and the context. We call this "topological alignment." Please note that there are two different contexts—one in which a student identifies and answers, and the second in which the student explains the answer.

Using the space provided, write down the content, context, and cognitive type of the test item.

My Deconstruction Analysis of the Florida Test Item

(Write your comments here.)

Content:

_____

_____

_____

_____

(Continued)

(Continued)

Context 1:

_____

_____

_____

_____

Context 2:

_____

_____

_____

_____

Cognitions Type:

_____

_____

_____

_____

Our analysis of the test item for content and context follows.
Content: Identify quadrilaterals and explain answer.
Context 1:

- Givens—Five different shapes, three of which are quadrilaterals; written directions for what to do
- Nature of Student Response—Circle the correct figures.
- Special vocabulary: Quadrilaterals

Cognition Type 1: Knowledge
Context 2:

- Givens—Same as Context 1 with added directions to explain answer; 3 lines on which to write.
- Nature of student response—Written
- Special Vocabulary—Same as Context 1

Cognition Type 2: Comprehension
If we were going to expand for deep alignment, we would do three things:

- Determine the range of content for this test item
- Identify the various types of contexts to which the content would be transferred
- Specify the various types of thinking cognition desired

For more information about how to achieve "deep alignment," please consult the deep alignment book by English and Steffy (2001). The key is to understand what is meant by "context" and the need for a teacher to use multiple contexts when teaching. In its completeness, Step 2 has three components as shown in Table 2.5.

Table 2.5   Three Components of Step 2

1. Derive the actual objective(s) taught (content, context, and cognitive type).
2. Observe for stated or listed objective (it might be on the board, the teacher might say it, it could be in a lesson plan that is open on the desk) and compare that with the observed objective for congruence.
3. Calibrate the actual objective taught.

In the second component of Step 2, we are not saying that the objective must be stated to the students or that it must be written on the board, though these are instructional decisions a teacher might make. The reason for identifying the objective is to compare what the teacher thinks he or she is teaching with what we observe is being taught. That is the extent of our observation. Some principals have misinterpreted this part of the five-step structure and turned it into, "The objective must be on the board." This is not our message. *Our message is that what the teacher thinks is being taught should be what is actually being taught.* It is about congruence.

Completed Step 2—Analysis of the Language Arts Lesson

Box 2.4   Language Arts Scenario—Step 2: Curriculum Decision Points

---

Part I: Actual Taught Objective

A. Content Taught:

Distinguish between an iambic and anapestic foot (syllables and stress) that might be used in a sonnet.

B. Context of the Taught Content:

- Given—Oral directions to describe differences or to clap
- Nature of the Student Response—Oral, hand clapping
- Special Vocabulary—Iambic, anapestic, sonnet

C. Cognitive Type: Knowledge

Part II: Listed or Stated Objective

Teacher stated the same objective as the observed objective. It is congruent with the objective actually taught.

Part III: Calibration

Course: 12th-grade English.

District Calibration: Located in the 7th-grade English curriculum course of the district curriculum [from a real district's curriculum scope and sequence: "Use iambic and anapestic feet in writing a sonnet."].

Think about your original analysis of this scenario. Did you even think about the curriculum? Often we find that observers go right for analyzing the instructional practices in their walk-throughs rather than thinking first about the curricular objective being taught. We have spent quite a bit of time describing Step 2 because it is often less practiced than the other steps.

Some of the district and/or state calibrations might be difficult to accomplish if only vague standards and objectives are mentioned, or if some standards are the same across grade levels. We find that principals using this process become advocates for a precise set of objectives by grade or course level, and for a feasible number of student learnings to be undertaken by teachers.

Some principals do "curriculum sweeps" when they first start using the process. They may go into the classroom to observe the objective(s) being taught; do calibrations; and prepare charts for grade level, department staff, and/or total staff review. Many principals/coaches do not try to do all of the 3 C's (content, context, and cognitive type) when they first work with our walk-through structure. We recommend getting the content down first, and only then moving to context and cognition type.

STEP 3: INSTRUCTIONAL DECISION POINTS

After we have derived the curriculum, we are ready to look at instructional teaching practices. Instructional practices are those practices a teacher uses to teach the objectives, such as questioning skills, use of non-linguistic representations, grouping strategies, and informal assessment strategies. (When you worked on the first scenario, you probably started your analysis with teacher practices.)

Step 3 consists of the components described in Table 2.6:

Table 2.6 Step 3 Components

- Determine the generic instructional decisions being made. Generic practices are those that could be used regardless of student age or subject area (e.g., comparing and contrasting, homework use, feedback, using examples, student error, non-linguistic representations, instruction at the right level of difficulty for each student, etc.).
- Identify strategies being used at a specific school and/or district focus. For instance, if the district has a goal of using reciprocal teaching or cooperative learning, the Marzano (2001) teaching skills, a principal would notice if and how these strategies were being used during the walk-through.
- Observe specific research-based, subject-specific practices, such as the use of meta-cognitive strategies, manipulatives, or mental computations in mathematics.

With our walk-through structure, it is important not to make judgments about the teaching practices, but rather to simply notice the instructional decisions being made. In reflective inquiry, a teacher is posed a question regarding the criteria he or she considers when selecting one instructional practice over another. Usually, by the time the principal has identified the curriculum objective(s), he or she has seen several instructional decisions and can leave the classroom.

We do not enter classrooms expecting to exit with an area for follow-up each time. In fact, with experienced teachers, we might have a follow-up conversation in the form of a reflective question once every two or three months, even though we are in their classrooms almost weekly. It is in the accumulation of data from multiple, brief visits that we begin to see patterns and identify possible areas for dialogue. In the interim, administrators are building a knowledge base about what students have learned as well as the instructional practices of the school across grades, courses, and teachers.

This process is not like a formal teacher evaluation observation in which administrators are trying to gather complete data and examine numerous instructional practices. At first, teachers will not understand why you are staying for such a short time and will think that you cannot see anything in such a short visit. One reason teachers ask you to stay longer is that they think you are judging their work. Over time they will realize that you are not in a judging mode but are in a coaching mode and that you do not need to examine every aspect of the teacher's teaching.

Recall the Language Arts scenario and what you saw. Did you mainly write down instructional practices?

Completed Step 3—Analysis of the Language Arts Lesson

Box 2.5   Language Arts Scenario—Step 3: Instructional Decision Points

---

Part I: Generic Instructional Practices

- Strategies for dealing with student error
- Approaches for having students let the teacher know their readiness to respond
- Variety of student response modes

Part II: School/District Focus

In the scenario, we don't know the school focus; none was provided.

Part III: Subject-Specific Instructional Practices

- Use of real-world experiences

Notice we listed only a few practices. You may have listed others. We do not need to see the same things. We are not judging the teacher's actions. The thoughts triggered in you may be different from another person's. In a real-life situation you will know the teacher, and you will have a better feeling for what might be a valuable area for reflective inquiry.

STEP 4: "WALK THE WALLS"—CURRICULAR AND INSTRUCTIONAL DECISIONS

You will almost always be able to complete Steps 1 through 3 of our walk-through structure. If you find that you identified the objective quickly and still have a little more time, you might want to look for learnings that have been taught or that might be taught in the future. We call this "walking the walls." You can observe many curricular objectives and instructional practices by noting what is on the wall as well as in other classroom locations.

It is strongly suggested that you do not start with this step, because you could use all your time on it without actually having observed the teaching decisions being rendered. Some principals do curriculum wall-walks after school with the teachers, carrying along the district curriculum objectives electronically or just the scope and sequence objectives in a chart form. Over time you will become accustomed to the walls in your classrooms, since teachers typically change only one of the sections at a time.

Mainly the walls reveal objectives. However, there may be instructional ideas on the walls, too. For instance, there may be procedure steps, such as the listing of the five parts of a descriptive essay and what goes into each paragraph. Or it might be a brainstormed list of synonyms that the students have completed as a class. (Displayed student projects with multiple names attached suggest small-group work.)

One of the interesting things to determine is why student work—celebrations, models, something from each student—is displayed. We have noticed often on our walk-throughs what we call "walls of humiliation." This is when every student's name is prominently posted on the wall with the number of books read, or the number of A's obtained, and so on. Occasionally we see postings of progress or semester grades listed by student I.D. An interesting reflective question for staff might be, "What criteria do you consider when deciding how the walls will be used as an extension of the learning environment?"

Besides the walls, there may be student portfolios or journals that could be reviewed to identify curriculum objectives. Worksheets on the teacher's desk or graded papers in a distribution box are student artifacts that would become part of our walk-the-walls step. Since we have no information relevant to this step in our scenario, we will not present an analysis for Step 4.

STEP 5: SAFETY AND HEALTH ISSUES

Step 5 just happens naturally. As you enter and exit classrooms, you will note particular safety or health issues. This is not a formal inspection or situation for placing blame; it is a time for making helpful observations. Some examples we have encountered include the following:

- Broken thresholds at entryways
- Extension cords and power strips creating a trip hazard
- Backpacks on floors in the aisles
- A student in a wheelchair located in the flow of traffic
- Dim or burned-out lights
- Air conditioning or blowers so loud you cannot hear the teacher
- Inadequate traffic flow because of the placement of tables and chairs
- A coffeemaker in a classroom, close to paper
- Paper and materials positioned precariously on top of tables, file cabinets, or bookshelves
- Lack of adequate ventilation
- Presence of chemical odors
- Paper cutter with a broken spring that allows the blade to fall freely

We are sure you could add to this list. Often we find that there are work orders that have been put on the back shelf that need to be brought forward. Since we have no information from our scenario relevant to this step, no analysis is provided for Step 5.

Now reflect on your approach as compared to our walk-through approach. Using the space provided, write down similarities and differences.

Pre/Post Comparisons Between My Walk-Through Thinking
and the Five-Step Process Described in This Chapter

Similarities and Differences

(Write your comments here.)

Similarities   Differences

_____

_____

_____

_____

How About Trying Out Our Five-Step Process?

The following is another walk-through observation scenario for you to consider. Read through the 6th-Grade Mathematics scenario and complete Steps 1 through 3 of your analysis on the worksheet.

Scenario Two: 6th-Grade Mathematics

[All students are looking at the teacher.]

Teacher: A percent means a part of 100. What is 30/100? [Teacher writes percent on the board.] [Three students raising their hands.] James?

James: 30 percent.

Teacher: Thank you. Any questions so far? [No hands go up.] What if I gave you 20/100? [Teacher writes percent on the board.] [Six students raising their hands.] Sally?

Sally: 20.

Teacher: 20 what?

Sally: 20 percent.

Teacher: Good. What if you have 7 out of 100? [Teacher writes percent on the board.] [Five students raising their hands.] Mark?

Mark: 7 percent.

Teacher: Thank you. What is this all leading to? Think for about 5 seconds. What am I trying to note? What if I had 100/100? [Teacher writes percent on the board.] What would this equal as a percent? [Five students raising their hands.] James?

James: 100 percent.

Teacher: Very good. Remember how ratios are a type of fraction. If I reduced 100/100 what would it be? [Teacher pointing to percent on the board.] [Five students raising their hands.] Mary?

Mary: 1.

Teacher: The whole number one equals 100 percent. If it is less than 100 percent it is a what?

Now it is time for you to do your analysis using the first three steps. Then we will give you our analysis.

Step 1: Student Orientation to the Work: _____

_____

Step 2: Curriculum Decision Points

Part I: Actual Observed Taught Curriculum

A. Content of the taught objective—Skill, knowledge, process, concept to be learned

_____

_____

B. Context of the taught objective—Conditions under which a student demonstrates the content
   • Givens: _____

_____

   • Nature of student response: _____

_____

- Vocabulary specific to the content: _____

_____

C. Cognitive Type—K, C, Ap, An, S, E _____

Part II: Stated or Observed Objective, if Easily Observed _____

_____

Part III: District Calibration (If you have your district curriculum, use it here.)

Step 3: Instructional Practice Decision Points

Part I: Generic Practices _____

_____

Part II: School/District Focus (Usc your district's or school's focus here.) _____

_____

Part III: Subject Area Practices _____

_____

The following is our analysis:

Step 1: Student Orientation to the Work:

Students oriented toward the teacher

Step 2: Curriculum Decision Points

Part I: Actual Observed Taught Curriculum

A. Content of the taught objective—Skill, knowledge, process, concept to be learned

- Convert simple fractions to percentages
- Convert fractions to whole numbers
- Convert whole numbers to percentages

(Continued)

(Continued)

B. Context of the taught objective—Conditions under which a student demonstrates the content

- Givens: Symbolic problems on the board, oral directions
- Nature of student response: Oral
- Vocabulary specific to the content: Ratio, fraction, whole number

C. Cognitive Type—Knowledge

Part II: Stated or Observed Objective, if Easily Observed

Nothing observed

Part III: District Calibration (If you have your district curriculum, use it here.)

3rd-grade objectives

Step 3: Instructional Practice Decision Points

Part I: Generic Practices

- Use of prior learning to transfer to new learnings
- Use of review
- Types of student responses
- Types of questions

Part II: School/District Focus (Use your district's or school's focus here.)

Not known

Part III: Subject Area Practices

- Metacognition
- Symbolic and real-world examples

A basic caution is in order here. We do not use any worksheet when conducting a walk-through in the classroom. Administrators must remember the components of the five-step process. It may take a few weeks of practice to internalize the steps. Until that time, the administrator may take a few notes, but very few, on a 3 × 5 card. (This technique will be described in detail in Chapter 5.)

SUMMARY

The flowchart in Table 2.7 is another view of the five-step structure:

Table 2.7   Five-Step Walk-Through Observation Structure

Curriculum	*Instruction*
	1. Student Orientation to Work

2. Objective (CCC)
  • Taught
  • Stated or Observed
  • District Calibration	

	3. Instructional Practices
	  • Generic
	  • School/District Focus
	  • Subject Specific

• Walk-the-Walls	
	5. Safety and Health

The major elements discussed in this chapter include the following:

- When conducting the walk-through, the principal is acting as a coach, gathering data about the decisions teachers are making regarding curriculum and instruction.
- We are not looking for strengths and weaknesses. We are not judging.
- We are not looking for areas to reinforce or refine, except with the novice teacher who needs our nurturing and instruction.
- We are looking for the curricular and instructional decision points the teacher is making.
- From an accumulation of visits, we consider teacher decision points that might be of value for the teacher to ponder.
- The major purpose of our walk-throughs is to provide opportunities for the teacher's professional growth. Professional growth is considered a process and not some abstract point of finality on a continuum of development.

Thinking back to the start of this chapter and your initial thoughts about walk-throughs and feedback, how has this chapter influenced your thoughts? Discuss your reflections with your learning partner, or think about them yourself and respond in the space provided.

Reflections on the Five-Step
Walk-Through Observation Structure

(Write your comments here.)

_____

_____

_____

_____

Moving Staff to Reflective Inquiry

Focusing on the Reflective Question and Conversation

The goal of follow-up conversations is to assist the teaching staff to engage in reflective inquiry. We use a differentiated coaching approach that moves teachers through dependent, independent, and interdependent stages—with the ultimate outcome being treating the teacher as a collegial participant in a collaborative interactive conversation. This chapter describes the details of the dependent-direct, independent-indirect, and interdependent-collaborative approaches. Key statements or questions are illustrated with a focus on the Downey Reflective Question and Conversation. Specific practice is given for the three approaches using the walk-through teaching scenarios that were analyzed in the previous chapter.

We propose an approach to follow-up conversations that departs from being direct and supervisor judged. We use a motivational approach because it dignifies individuals through professional conversations. We believe the role of the principal will change, based on these different types of follow-up conversations. The word "feedback" is used only for the direct interaction. Table 3.1 serves as an advanced organizer for this chapter (see Downey & Frase, 2001).

Seldom do we suggest that you leave a note regarding your observations, other than for the novice/apprentice teacher who is typically at a dependent stage and needs nurturing and positive reinforcement. For this

Table 3.1   Follow-Up Conversation and Dialogue Paradigm for Walk-Through

Dependent (Direct)	Supervisor/coach gives feedback to teacher and then *teaches* the teacher in the feedback conversation.
Independent (Indirect)	Supervisor/coach invites teacher to reflect on the short segment of observed teaching and follows up on those teaching practices that the teacher brings up, and hopefully finishes the conversation with a reflective question.
Interdependent (Collegial)	Supervisor/coach poses reflective question in a conversation and engages in further dialogue in the future if teacher so chooses.

purpose, we briefly describe the components of a quality note in this chapter.

Remember, this book is not about dealing with marginal employees. However, a direct and frank approach is used along with specific behaviors to be changed when dealing with such individuals.

Before you read the content of this chapter, please refer back to the lesson scenarios in Chapter 2 on the walk-through observational structure— the English and mathematics scenarios. For one of the two teachers, identify a possible curricular or instructional teaching practice for which you might leave a positive note of reinforcement or have a follow-up conversation. Write the curricular or instructional practice in the space provided.

Curricular or Instructional Teaching Practice for Note and/or Possible Follow-Up Conversation With One of the Teachers

(Write your comments here.)

_____

_____

_____

_____

Table 3.2   Flow of Supervisor/Employee Relationships

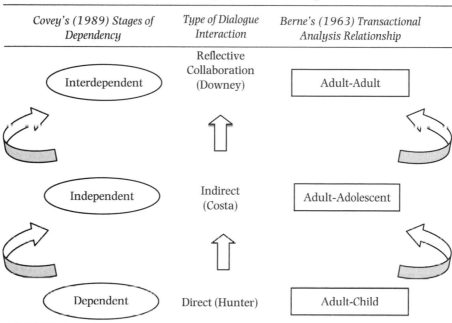

Covey's (1989) Stages of Dependency	Type of Dialogue Interaction	Berne's (1963) Transactional Analysis Relationship
Interdependent	Reflective Collaboration (Downey)	Adult-Adult
Independent	Indirect (Costa)	Adult-Adolescent
Dependent	Direct (Hunter)	Adult-Child

You will use the above information later as you go through this chapter. You will be asked to write a note showing how you would respond to three different types of follow-up conversation interactions as illustrated in Table 3.2—direct, indirect, and collaborative.

HOW DO WE PROVIDE DIRECT FEEDBACK?

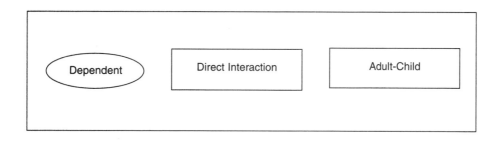

Many of us have provided direct feedback to teachers about their practice. This is the style of management that has been used by most administrators and coaches over the years. It is a comfortable style because of its familiarity. This section first discusses whether to leave notes or not and then goes on to describe the process of using direct feedback that assists the teacher to engage in reflection.

The Note

One of the main ways of providing direct feedback is through notes. For years many administrators and teachers thought a note needed to be left in every classroom visited. In fact, if a note was not left, administrators felt guilty. Not now! We suggest you visit classrooms often, and leave few notes.

Here is a new procedure for you to consider. First, leave few notes, except for the novice/apprentice teacher or an observed "Herculean effort" on the part of a teacher. Notes are a one-way type of communication. They are adult-child communications—*bosslike.* You (the boss) *tell* the teachers (the employees) what you think about their work. This is hierarchical in nature, and, if we are not careful, reinforces the boss-employee relationship rather than encouraging the collaborative interaction we desire. It is a dependency-inducing strategy.

Blase and Blase (1998) report that teachers love notes. Probably the reason they like for us to leave notes is their desire for external affirmation of their work. Our approach is to move teachers to self-affirmation and to move staff away from needing our approval. These dependency environments are created over time through the vertical chain of command that is the hallmark of school bureaucracies. Such environments are often restrictive and do not provide for creativity of thought—employees always needing to get the "boss's" approval. We advocate leaving fewer notes and using strategies that move individuals to a sense of self-affirmation rather than a sense of being "other-affirmed." You are not after a dependency mentality on the part of teachers, who would then end up constantly needing your approval for their work. When you maintain this type of relationship, you will probably never be able to give enough accolades to satisfy your teachers.

When notes are used, mainly for novice/apprentice teachers, they need to be in the form of positive reinforcement. Such teachers need encouragement and nurturing as well as lots of suggestions for growth. Unfortunately, we have experienced many situations where principals choose to leave notes on "areas that need improvement." Many staff members misread these words, and such approaches often push teachers away and keep supervisors from being a good influence in their careers. We strongly suggest that if you are going to make recommendations for "improvements needed," you do it in a conversation.

Using the example of one of the teachers highlighted in the Chapter 2 scenarios, write a positive reinforcement note to the teacher and then analyze the note in terms of its attributes. Pretend each is a beginning teacher.

```
                        Positive Note for Teacher

 (Write your comments here.)

 _____

 _____

 _____

 _____
```

Here are some components of a sample reinforcement note:

Table 3.3   Ingredients of a Quality Positive Note

- Is *descriptive* about a specific teaching practice (curriculum or instruction)
- Notes *effect of the teaching practice* on student learning/behavior
- Presents a *rationale/research* for using the behavior (if possible)
- Encourages teacher to *continue* the practice and to reflect about the decisions a teacher makes regarding when to use the practice
- Is *genuine,* and seen as sincere by the teacher
- Is *positive* in tone

Here are two examples of positive notes for the two teachers in scenarios from Chapter 2:

12th-Grade English Teacher:

You used several effective approaches for providing a risk-free environment for student responses, i.e., raised hand and formation of the hand—open, closed, cupped. Such strategies increased student willingness to participate and to try to answer the question. Continue to use such strategies and to reflect on how you decide which strategies to use and when. Loved being in your classroom today.

6th-Grade Mathematics Teacher:

Your style is so helpful for students. One of the strategies you use is to allow wait time after your questions. Such an approach gives each student a chance to prepare a response before the answer is given. This increases learning through additional practice opportunities. Keep up the good work and think about how you decide when to use wait time, and when you do use it, how much wait time to provide.

Go back now and examine your note in comparison with the examples above, and see what components of a quality reinforcement note you included.

A Better Approach—Discussion

Now that the strategy of leaving a note has been described, let us be clear that *a better approach to feedback is dialogue.* The note is a one-way communication. It seldom provides dialogue except when a teacher feels compelled to come and speak to you about it. *Two-way interactions* help clarify ideas, influence thought, and allow you to see the teacher's reaction to your ideas. A note seldom stretches a person's cognitive field. It is about something already accomplished. It feels good for a short while, but it is merely an event; it comes from the top down, and then it is over. Our goal is to continue reflective inquiry about a teacher's practice over time. It is to be a journey of thought, not an event. As mentioned in Chapter 1, our goal is to influence the teacher's reflections to promote future action; it is not about reflection on the past. It is to encourage a proactive rather than reactive type of reflection. A note is almost always written about past practice and infrequently moves a teacher to change future action.

Glasser (1992), in his book *The Quality School,* distinguishes between the "boss manager" and the "lead manager." The boss manager uses traditional methods of motivation. Such a manager is interested only in short-term compliance and is seldom interested in long-term growth. The lead manager is the individual who facilitates employees in being responsible for their own assessment and who focuses on their personal and professional growth. The idea in our walk-through is to function as a lead manager.

Direct Feedback Statement and Conversation

If you adopt a direct approach in providing feedback, the interactive style is preferred. When you are in this role, you are in a mentoring and teaching role. You are bringing to the surface something you wish the teacher to consider in his or her practice.

The direct approach is mainly used with novice/apprentice teachers as they grow in their practice, or when dealing with classroom management (Step 1) or safety or health issues (Step 5).

Rather than pose a question to a teacher with whom you wish to be direct, form a focused statement on the teaching practice you wish to discuss. For example:

Instead of Asking	*Make a Statement*
How do you decide when to use wait time, and how long to wait?	I would like to chat with you about wait time—how you decide when to use it and when not to use it and how long to wait.
How do you decide which objectives to teach to which students?	I would like to talk with you today about the selection of objectives to teach—and which students are taught which objectives.

When you wish to make a direct statement, don't use the interrogatory form. If you have something to declare, say it! A question may put the person on the spot. Novice/apprentice teachers often are not quite sure what to answer, and experienced teachers may say a lot, often in a defensive manner. Teachers feel obligated to answer such direct questions, and then the answers may put you in a defensive conversation or move the conversation in a different direction than desired.

For example, a teacher might say in response to a question about the use of wait time, "Today I started to use wait time and then decided from the looks in their eyes that they might not know the answer. So I cut short the wait time and began to cue students to the answer." Now what do you say? The focus has shifted to today's lesson and is no longer on the general criteria a teacher uses to make decisions about wait time. Depending upon the tone of the teacher, you might have to stop to deal with the fact that the teacher responded in a defensive way. Making statements rather than asking questions is a hallmark of being direct and guides the discussion in the direction you desire—also, it may avoid putting the teacher in a potentially defensive posture.

Initially, you may find making direct statements difficult. Using questions may be more comfortable, but they are usually about the past. For instance, note the following examples:

- "How do you know the students learned what you wanted them to learn?"
- "How did you decide to teach this particular objective today?"
- "Why did you decide to use this particular activity?"

These questions seldom move a teacher to reflective inquiry. What they portend is answering the supervisor or coach about past practice.

Here is a different way to express the same ideas through a statement that could then be followed up with either coaching or reflection:

- "Let's talk about how we set up evaluation processes to determine which students are learning the objectives we want them to learn."
- "I would like us to think about how we select objectives from the district curriculum to be at the right level of difficulty for students to challenge them in their learning."
- "I would like to chat with you about the criteria we use to select one activity over another when teaching the district's curriculum."

Notice that the statements are direct but much softer in tone. Furthermore, the statements provide more detail about the direction of the forthcoming conversation. Posing a question to a teacher at the dependent level—a teacher who is probably doing the best he or she knows how—could embarrass the individual. Our goal is to act as coaches who attempt to influence thinking, and embarrassment moves the person away from us rather than toward us.

As an exercise, for each one of the teacher scenarios in Chapter 2, write a statement that could be included in a direct-feedback conversation you might have with the teacher. Use the area of follow-up you (and your learning partner) selected earlier in your reading of this chapter.

Direct Statement for the Language Arts Teacher

(Write your statement here.) _____

_____

_____

Direct Statement for the Mathematics Teacher

(Write your statement here.) _____

_____

_____

Here are some examples of statements. Compare these with what you wrote:

Language Arts Teacher:

"Let's think together about decisions one makes regarding the nature of the student responses for various types of learning."

"I would like to chat with you about how you decide when to and when not to deal with student error, and if you choose to deal with it, the strategies you consider employing."

Mathematics Teacher:

"Let's talk about practice strategies we might use in reviewing prior learnings to link them to a new learning."

"I would like to chat with you about checking-for-understanding strategies that provide the opportunity for each student to prepare a response and respond, thus giving students more practice on the learning."

Notice in the examples that although the statement is direct, there are no judgmental words—either positive or negative. Even when being direct, you want to move teachers to reflective thought about the decisions they are making. Your statements are neutral and businesslike in nature. The focus is on the curricular or instructional teaching practice decisions, not on the teacher behavior observed in the walk-through.

We do not equate being direct with reinforcing or refining areas of teacher behavior. Certainly a note is reinforcing when you leave a statement about something the teacher did that was effective from your perspective. We wish to be very careful about to whom and how often we leave such notes. They reinforce the hierarchical structure and might perpetuate a dependency environment. In your conversations you may choose to use refinement or reinforcing statements, but do so infrequently. You will need to use more reinforcement with novice/apprentice teachers. However, the goal ultimately is to move people to self-affirmation.

If there truly is something the novice teacher needs to change, then say this very directly. For instance, "I expect you to use all of the instructional time available for learning. You have too much down time when students are not working. I would like to talk about strategies for engaging students almost all of the time during the day." Notice the strong statements. Seldom would a supervisor need to use this direct an approach; it would be used only in classroom situations where teacher performance is potentially marginal.

Table 3.4   Conversation Attributes and Sequence for Direct-Dependent
                  Feedback

1. Set a time frame for the conversation.

2. Reinforce how the teacher tends to be a reflective person.

3. Give a focused statement on the teaching practice to be addressed.

4. Invite the teacher to reflect with you.

5. Briefly describe the behavior observed in the walk-through and the
    decision to be made, and then state the curricular or instructional practice
    into which this decision fits.

6. Talk about the teaching practice.

7. Incorporate research.

8. Check for understanding.

9. End with a reflective question to continue thought on the curricular or
    instructional teaching practice.

10. Exit quickly.

The direct statement is not made in a vacuum. There will be a
conversation that goes on around the statement. A proposed conversation
sequence is shown in Table 3.4.

Notice that in the conversational sequence you are expected to talk
(Step 6). We often call this "teaching the teacher" and sometimes refer to
it as "teach the teaching practice." This individual is dependent upon you
for knowing what to do; this is why you are being direct. Be careful not to
give too many ideas when you talk—base this upon the experience level of
the teacher and your relationship with him or her.

The direct conversation takes more time than the reflective conversation, which will be discussed later in this chapter. Usually 10 to 15 minutes
of time is needed to provide this type of direct feedback and to move to the
reflective question. Set a time frame when you begin your conversation,
and then just a minute before you need to leave, say so and move out
quickly. Teachers are very busy people. As Fenwick English (2001) has
stated, "There are three things we know about teachers. First, they are
very busy. Second, they are very busy. And third, they are very busy." We
must honor their time and ours.

Table 3.5 is an example of how the conversation might proceed
(coach's statements only), along with the attributes of the conversation.
Notice how the idea of reflective inquiry is woven throughout the
following dialogue, even as the supervisors are being direct.

Table 3.5   Example of Direct-Dependent Conversation From Coach's Perspective With Attributes of Conversation (Does not include teacher comments.)

What the Coach Might Say	Attributes
Have you got about ten minutes? I wanted to give you some feedback from my observation today.	Set time line.
I know you like to think about the teaching art and about your teaching decisions. I have an idea for you to think about.	Reinforce reflection.
Today I would like to talk with you about the decisions we make regarding the use of wait time—when to use it, how to set it up, and length of wait time.	Give a focused statement on instructional teaching practice to be addressed.
Think with me about how you make decisions about wait time.	Invite teacher to reflect with you.
How I came to think about this was that I briefly observed and saw that today you used wait time in your lesson. You had asked a question about what the percent of the fraction 20/100 was. You said, "I am going to give you five seconds to think about your answer." Let's think about what criteria we use to decide whether or not to use wait time and how long wait time should be."	Briefly describe behavior observed in the walk-through and the decision that led to a particular teaching practice.
Let's start with how we decide to use wait time. It is a very effective strategy that is used quite often. Think with me about how we decide to use it. Here are some times when we might use it: (give a couple of examples and encourage the teacher to add ideas.)	Teach—supervisor teaches teacher the concept. (Interaction is important here.)

- Acquisition of new learning
- Checking for understanding
- Initial oral practice
- After an error has taken place

Here is when we would probably not want to use it:

- Desiring fluidity of response
- Want automatic response

(Continued)

Table 3.5 (Continued)

What the Coach Might Say	*Attributes*
Calling on students is best done when the question is posed to the entire class and only after allowing students time to think. It is essential that you pose questions in such a way that you expect every student to be responsible for an answer (Downey, 2002).	
If a student is called on before the question is posed, all other students can choose to not think about the answer. Or, if you call on a student too quickly after the question, you get the same results.	
Allowing time to think is a critical aspect of learning. Any response by a student before the other students are able to think about the answer immediately stops any further pondering or reflection on their part.	
How long do you wait after a question before having students respond? Most teachers do not wait long enough—sometimes only one second before calling on a student. Research has shown that most teachers find it difficult to wait, but when they do, it is related to higher student achievement.	
How much time should you wait? This is a hard question to answer—it depends on so many variables—level of difficulty of the question, prior experience with the content, just to name two. We probably would want to wait around 10 seconds before we ask for a response to most questions. Count to 10.	
The value of wait time is that it provides each student an opportunity to think about an answer before another student gives the answer. It provides practice opportunities. Some students need more time than others to come up with the answer, and this provides equity of response opportunity.	Incorporate research.
Rowe, as described by Good and Brophy (2000), found that teachers who extended their wait times to three to five seconds found an	

- Increase in the average length of student responses
- Increase in unsolicited but appropriate student responses
- Decrease in failures to respond
- Increase in speculative responses
- Increase in student-to-student comparisons of data
- Increase in statements that involved drawing inferences from evidence
- Increase in student-initiated questions
- A greater variety of contributions by students.

Think about tomorrow's lesson and some questions you might ask. Let's practice with you setting up the question with wait time; pretend I am a student.	Check for understanding.
So keep thinking about this idea of wait time. When you are teaching and asking questions, as well as thinking about when to provide wait time and how much time to give, what criteria do you use to make these wait time decisions, to provide each student the opportunity to learn the objectives?	End with reflective question to continue thought on teaching practice.
Need to leave. If you wish to chat more about this give me a call or e-mail.	Exit quickly.

Obviously, this would not be just a one-way conversation; the teacher dialogue was not included. The key to being direct, however, is that you put yourself into a teaching mode. If the teacher already knew what you wanted him or her to think about, you would not need to be direct.

Your knowledge of the research on curricular and instructional practices needs to be thorough. (In the bibliography at the back of this book, several resources are listed that you might want to have in your professional library to help you in this area.)

Now it is time to practice the direct-feedback approach. Using a focused statement from one of the teachers in the scenarios, write a sample conversation in the space provided in the left-hand column.

Form 3.1

Practice on Being Direct	
(Outline your comments in the left-hand column.)	
What You Would Say	**Attributes**
	Set time frame.
	Reinforce reflection.
	State focused; direct statement on curricular or instructional teaching practice to be addressed.
	Invite the teacher to reflect with you.
	Briefly describe the behavior observed in the walk-through and the decision the teacher made leading to the teaching practice.
	Teach about the curricular or instructional teaching practice. (Interaction is important here.)
	Incorporate research.
	Check for understanding.
	End with reflective question to continue thought on teaching practice.
	Exit quickly.

HOW DO WE PROVIDE INDIRECT
OPPORTUNITIES FOR REFLECTIVE INQUIRY?

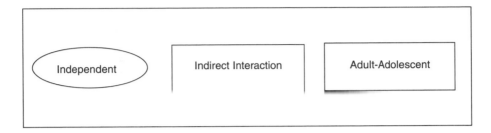

If you determine that the teacher is at the independent level, our approach is to invite reflection. It is the teacher's choice whether to dialogue with you or not. Remember, this process is to be used with a satisfactorily performing individual. Such individuals appear to be confident in their teaching and are fairly independent in their work. Their relationship with you is one of confidence. It is important to note that in some cases the teacher may not be very receptive to the conversation. However, most teachers will be polite. Our goal remains to help the teacher reflect on his or her practice and, hopefully, to move him or her to the interdependent stage by ending with a reflective question about some teaching practice brought up in the conversation.

You need to be in these teachers' classrooms as often as others on the faculty. Just your presence alone will influence their thinking. Then, occasionally be in a place where you can casually ask them if they wish to reflect on their practices. Do this after a brief walk-through where things seemed to be working fine. Invite reflection. If they say "no" or indicate they have other tasks, smile and say "fine" in a positive tone and move on. However, you will probably find that the teacher will be responsive to you. In these situations, always keep the conversation positive. Even if you have something you would like to bring up that might be an area for refinement, "zip the lip." You are trying to help the teacher be reflective and eventually develop a collegial relationship with you.

Use the reflective thinking ideas of Costa (1994) here. Be very indirect. Invite reflection. Make an unfocused statement. For instance, "Things seemed to be working well for you today in your classroom." Do not focus on a particular teaching practice. The suggested attributes and sequence of this conversation are listed in Table 3.6.

Table 3.6   Conversation Attributes and Sequence for Indirect-Independent Invitation for Reflection

1. Set a time frame for the conversation (three to four minutes).

2. Make a positive statement about the classroom situation observed.

3. Invite reflection in a general way.

4. Ask an unfocused question about the classroom situation.

5. Probe for the criteria the teacher uses in making a particular decision when one is brought up—a type of reflective question.

6. Exit quickly with a comment of a reflective nature regarding the teaching practice mentioned by the teacher and add an invitation for follow-up if desired.

Table 3.7 is an example of how the conversation might proceed (coach's statements only) along with the attributes of the conversation.

Table 3.7   Example of Indirect-Independent Invitation to Reflective Conversation. From Coach's Perspective With Attributes of Conversation (Does not include teacher comments.)

What the Coach Might Say	*Attributes*
Hi. Do you have you about three to four minutes to chat? (If no, say "fine" and move on.)	Set time frame of conversation
When I walked through your room, it seemed like . . . (one of following) . . . the lesson was going well for you. . . . students were learning what you wanted them to. . . . your actions were bringing about desired student behavior.	Make a positive statement about the classroom situation.
I know you enjoy reflecting on your work; would you like to take a couple of minutes to think about your practices? (If yes, continue.)	Invite reflection in a general way.
When you think about this lesson, what decisions were you making that seemed to be working well for you with the students? (Often teachers are descriptive here and keep trying to turn the conversation to decisions.)	Ask an unfocused question about the classroom situation.

Very interesting, so one of the areas you make decisions on is [teaching practice brought up by the teacher]. When you are planning or delivering your instruction and thinking about [practice], what criteria do you use to decide when and how to use [the practice] to help students in their learning.

Probe for criteria teacher uses in making a particular decision when it is brought up—a type of reflective question.

Got to run, see you later. Keep reflecting on decisions in the area of [practice]. If you want to chat further, let me know.

Exit quickly with a comment of a reflective nature on the teaching practice mentioned by the teacher and an invitation for follow-up, if desired.

Now it is time for you to practice the indirect, yet invitational, conversation approach. Decide on a curricular or instructional teaching practice for one of your teachers; now write out the conversation.

Form 3.2

Practice on Being Indirect—Inviting Reflective Inquiry	
(Outline your comments in the left-hand column.)	
What You Would Say	**Attributes**
	Set time frame of conversation.
	Make a positive statement about the classroom situation.
	Invite reflection in a general way.

(Continued)

Form 3.2 (Continued)

Practice on Being Indirect Reflective Inquiry	
(Outline your comments in the left-hand column.)	
What You Would Say	**Attributes**
	Ask an unfocused question about the classroom situation.
	Probe for criteria teacher uses in making a particular decision when it is brought up—a type of reflective question.
	Exit quickly with a comment of a reflective nature on the teaching practice mentioned by the teacher and an invitation for follow-up, if desired.

HOW DO WE ASK REFLECTIVE QUESTIONS AND CARRY ON THE CONVERSATION?

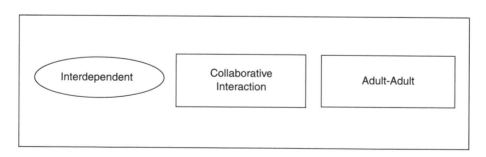

Ultimately, the goal is to move all staff to the level of collegial collaboration and interaction. This section presents the reflective question first and then provides you with examples and practice. Then a conversation will be presented in which a reflective question is embedded. It is not difficult to come up with a reflective question once you practice it, but because it is so different from how we normally interact with teachers, you might find yourself stumbling at first.

THE REFLECTIVE QUESTION

How do we ask the reflective question? A reflective question was presented earlier in the section where direct conversation was described. The conversation ended with a reflective question. The topic was the instructional practice of using wait time. Here is that example again:

> *"When you are teaching and asking questions*
> *and thinking about when to provide wait time and how much time to give*
> *what criteria do you use*
> *to make these wait-time decisions*
> *to provide each student the opportunity to learn the objectives?"*

The above question is about an *instructional decision* by the teacher. Here is an example of a reflective question about a *curriculum decision* a teacher might make:

> *"When you are planning your units of study*
> *and thinking about the selection of objectives to build into such units*
> *how do you decide among all the objectives you could teach*
> *which objectives to teach*
> *to move students forward in their learning?"*

It is important to recognize that we *do not write reflective questions*. The two examples above show how the reflective question might be posed orally—as a group of phrases in a conversation. The questions would be too long and too complex to write them the way we speak. You will notice, they are written here in five lines; this is because there are five essential elements to the reflective question. More about that later as well as a description of how we put the question into a conversation.

First, examine the attributes of the reflective question that are presented in Table 3.8.

Here are several points regarding these attributes using the example reflective questions:

- *Decision:* The coach is not the decision maker; the teacher is the decision maker. Include language like "in deciding" or "to decide" in the question. How to teach is the teacher's decision, not yours.

Table 3.8   Attributes of a Reflective Question

Decision *(How do you decide)*
Choice *(Criteria used)*
About one's practice, not about the lesson observed—Reflection for action, not reflection on past actions *(Use present tense)*
Many situations/contexts *(Plural)*
Analysis, synthesis, or evaluation cognitive thinking Neutral/Non-judgmental *(Neither positive nor negative in tone)*
Positive presuppositions *(Assumes person is thinking about and doing what is presented in the question)*
Honor what was observed *(If possible)*
Impact on student learning *(Cause-and-effect analysis)*
Seen as substantive and meaningful *(Teacher sees it as valuable)*

However, we do not start our reflective question with these statements. There are several phrases that come earlier.

- *Choice:* The choice attribute comes out in questions such as, "What criteria do you use?" or "Among all the things you could have decided, what influenced you?" Choice is powerful. Choosing what to teach is not the coach's choice; it is the teacher's choice. We want the teacher to reflect on the choices he or she is making. When we combine elements of choice and decision in the same question, we move the teacher to a higher cognitive level of analysis and synthesis. If you simply ask, "How do you decide . . ." without mentioning or implying choice, you are asking for a comprehension level of thought. The coach raises the level of thoughtful reflection by asking the teacher to think about the criteria being used to make the decisions the teacher *chooses to make.*

- *About One's Practice:* Most of us are used to making comments or asking questions about the lesson we observed. The reflective question we are proposing in this approach is not about the lesson. Observing the lesson just helps us to look at decision patterns of the teacher and triggers us to cite something we think could be of value for the teacher to consider. Ask about the decisions the teacher is making or might make in the future, not about decisions that have already been made. We want reflection *for* action, not reflection *on* action. This is a very difficult habit for many supervisors/coaches to break. If you hear yourself asking a question in the past tense, you are probably discussing the lesson. Speak in the present tense—rather than "How *did* you decide?" say "How *do* you decide?" The starter phrase of your question is impacted here as well and should also be in the present tense, for example, "When you are planning your lessons . . ." "When you are teaching . . ." and "When you are evaluating your student achievement . . ."

- *Many Situations/Contexts:* There seldom is a right or wrong practice. Correctness is dependent on context, and there are so many contexts in which a teacher is making decisions. Be very careful about your choice of words, and put your language in plural form—for example "lessons," "units of study," "among the various situations you find yourself in," so as not to single out any particular context.

- *Analysis, Synthesis, or Evaluative Cognitive Thinking:* By placing the teacher in a specific context and asking him or her about the criteria for decision making, the reflective question prompts him or her to consider a response using advanced cognitive levels. For example, "When you are planning your lessons and thinking about the approaches you might use to evaluate student learning, what criteria do you use in selecting those approaches?" calls for analytical thinking; whereas a question such as "How did you select the evaluation approaches you used in this lesson?" calls for comprehension-level thinking (Bloom et al., 1956).

- *Neutral/Nonjudgmental:* This is a tricky area for us and often for staff. We are accustomed to making judgment statements, and teachers expect them. They sound like, "I liked the way you . . ." or "That strategy you used today was excellent." Other examples are, "A strategy you might want to consider might be . . ." or "One way to do this is . . ." Certainly these phrases could be used when you want to be direct (first stage). But when you want to encourage the highest level of reflective inquiry, your judgment is not relevant. It is *the teacher's reflection* that is critical. Try not to come off as judgmental; be neither positive nor negative. When you are desirous of being at the collaborative-interdependent level, you want to sound neutral. It sounds like, "As you are planning your lessons around the curriculum, and thinking about a particular practice . . ." You will need to work with teachers so that they understand what you are doing, because even the most experienced teachers expect your praise. We want teachers to become *self*-affirmed, not *other*-affirmed—they should break free of being dependent upon our affirmation of their work. Of course, there will be times when you will want or need to praise, but these times should be infrequent.

- *Positive Presuppositions (assumes person is thinking about and doing what is presented in the question):* This is a very important attribute of the reflective question. Stating that the teacher is already thinking about some practice, establishes the belief that it is important. Moreover, it establishes high expectations. It also moves the conversation to an adult-adult dialogue as opposed to encouraging a dependency response. The positive presuppositions can occur at the start of the reflective question and throughout the reflective question. For example, "When you are planning your lessons around the district curriculum . . ." strongly implies that the district curriculum should be critical to the person's thinking. Another example, " . . . and thinking about the types of questions you might ask around the lesson objectives . . ." indicates that one believes the teacher is already thinking about these types of instructional situations. In fact, each one of the five elements of the reflective question is a positive presupposition.

- *Honor What Was Observed:* This one is ticklish because you do not want to discuss the lesson. You can include in the question something you observed, but you need to include other examples as well. For instance, in the wait time question, we did include a description of what we saw, but we also asked about when and when not to use wait time.

- *Impact on Student Learning:* End the reflective question with an "effect" statement. The goal is for teachers to always be analyzing the decisions they make *(cause)* to see the impact those decisions have on student learning *(effect)*. Eliciting effect is shown in the two examples using the phrases, "to move students forward in their learning" and "to provide each student the opportunity to learn the objectives."

- *Seen as Substantive and Meaningful:* This attribute is not in the reflective question itself, but relates to Chapter 2 where we discuss how you make decisions about what you bring to the teacher for reflection in the first place. It is important that teachers value the question and find it meaningful. This is such a critical attribute. It makes more difference motivationally that you select a teacher-valued area of reflection than the actual teaching practice itself. The goal is conscious reflection when making any teaching decision. This is so important that it was included here as a critical attribute of a reflective question/conversation.

Here are two reflective question examples—one a *curriculum teaching practice* and one an *instructional teaching practice.*

Curriculum Decision

"As you plan your lessons around the district's curriculum,
and if you are desirous of integrating objectives from other disciplines into
your lessons some of the time,
what factors do you consider
in deciding which curricular objectives to use across various disciplines
in order to provide efficiency in student learning of the objectives?"

Instructional Decision

"In planning your lessons around the district curriculum,
and in thinking about activities you might use,
what thoughts go on in your mind about
which activities to select
to impact student achievement?"

Table 3.9 presents questions that do not meet the attributes described, along with the reasons why:

Table 3.9 Questions and Missing Attributes

Questions	Missing Attributes
How did you decide whether the students achieved the objectives of the lesson?	• Fails to set up the situation wherein the teacher makes the decision; fails to focus on the criteria used.
What other strategies have you considered using in keeping students actively engaged in the lesson?	• Choice (*which ones to use and when*) • Many contexts • Cognitive thinking (*requests comprehension response*)
You use many fine approaches to create a readiness for the student to learn; how do you decide which type of approach to use?	• Neutral/Nonjudgmental (leads off with a *positive statement*)

Examine the questions below and write down what you think might be the missing attributes.

Form 3.3

Read Question	Missing Attributes
How did you select the objectives for this lesson?	
How do you decide when and when not to use wait time?	
When you are in teaching situations and thinking about how you will have students respond to your questions, how do you decide which approach to use?	

Here are the answers:

Questions	*Missing Attributes*
How did you select the objectives for this lesson?	• Choice • Many situations/contexts • Cognitive thinking type • Positive presuppositions • Fails both to set up the situation under which the teacher makes the decision and to focus on the criteria used • Impact on student learning

Questions	Missing Attributes
How do you decide when and when not to use wait time?	Same as above
When you are in teaching situations and thinking about how you will have students respond to your questions, how do you decide which approach to use?	• Choice • Cognitive thinking type • Impact on student learning

Here are some phrases to avoid because they tend to move you away from including all the critical attributes of a reflective question (Downey & Frase, 2001). Notice how many of them are past tense as well.

- Why did you do . . . ?
- Have you considered doing . . . ?
- You might want to . . .
- How come you . . . ?
- What might you do differently next time?
- How did you decide . . . ?
- Tell me how you did . . .
- How do you know that . . . ?
- Do you think it would have been different if you . . . ?

These are typical phrases that we use when discussing lessons observed during walk-throughs; however, they will seldom lead to reflective inquiry. Rather, they call for an immediate response of knowledge or cognitive thinking.

To move the teacher to reflective inquiry, we use a question that includes five elements. Table 3.10 presents an example with these elements:

Table 3.10 Five Elements of a Reflective Question (With Example)

Question Elements	Curriculum Example
1. Situation (and possible condition)	"When planning your lessons from the district standards . . .
2. Teacher reflection on curricular or instructional teaching practice	. . . and thinking about which objectives you will teach at any given point in time and in which order . . .

(Continued)

Table 3.10 (Continued)

Question Elements	Curriculum Example
3. Choice	. . . what criteria do you use . . .
4. Decision, and brings back the teaching practice in a general way	. . . to decide which objectives you will teach . . .
5. Student impact	. . . in order to have a high probability of students achieving the learnings you desire?

Question Elements	Instructional Example
1. Situation (and possible condition)	"When planning your lessons around the district curriculum . . .
2. Teacher reflection on curricular or instructional teaching practice	. . . and thinking about the learning activities you might select to teach the objectives . . ."
3. Choice	. . . what thoughts go on in your mind . . .
4. Decision, and brings back the teaching practice in a general way	. . . about which of the activities to select . . .
5. Student impact	. . . to have a high likelihood that each student learns the objectives?"

It is important to use the five elements in the sequence proposed to ensure that the positive presuppositions are in place and so that you move the teacher to enhanced analytical thought.

As you will notice, you should always start out by identifying the *situation*, for example,

- When you are planning your lessons . . .
- When you are teaching . . .
- When you are evaluating your teaching . . .

Often as a part of this statement you may add a condition; for instance,

- . . . around the district curriculum standards . . .
- . . . for students who are bilingual . . .
- . . . for students who have great variability in their pre-entry level skills . . .

Then, and this is very critical, follow this with the *teacher thinking and teaching practice*—curriculum or instructional. Start this part of your reflective question with the word *and*. Most people want to move right into the *why, why not, how, when* words here. If you do this, you will move your reflective question to a comprehension level. Here are some examples of how best to say this:

1. . . . *and* thinking about which objectives you might teach in a given unit of study . . .

2. . . . *and* considering the many possible types of questions you might ask . . .

3. . . . *and* wondering about how you might gather data about the current knowledge of the student through assessment approaches . . .

4. . . . *and* thinking about when you might want to use metacognitive strategies in the lessons . . .

After you have identified the situation and the teaching thinking and practice, you now will use your *choice* element. It is often useful to start with the word "what." Here are some example phrases that put *choice* before decisions:

1. what criteria do you use . . .

2. what factors do you consider . . .

3. what thoughts go on in your head . . .

4. what considerations do you make . . .

Follow this with the *decision element*—typically by using a phrase such as "to decide." At this time you should also mention the teaching practice involved, as discussed in detail earlier. Here are some example phrases:

1. . . . to decide on the objectives to be taught . . .

2. . . . to decide on the questions . . .

3. . . . to decide on the assessment approaches . . .

4. . . . in making decisions on when to use the strategies . . .

End the reflective question with some *student impact* phrases such as the following:

- . . . to impact student achievement?
- . . . to increase the likelihood of student mastery?
- . . . to assist each student in learning the objectives?

The reason for including the teaching practice right after the situation is that it sets up the positive presupposition and also makes the question more neutral. If you place the teaching practice *after* the words "what criteria do you use," you are more apt to have a type of "interrogation" question—a question often seen as negative by the teacher and one that has to be answered to the "boss."

Here are some sample curriculum reflective questions (Downey & Frase, 2001) that, *when stated orally,* would meet our criteria:

Curriculum Example	*Question Elements*
When planning out a semester of work or a project in which you will not have the time to teach all of the state standards expected . . .	1. *Situation and possible condition*
. . . AND thinking about the selection of objectives for different levels of students . . .	2. *Teacher reflection on curricular or instructional teaching practice*
. . . what criteria do you use . . .	3. *Choice*
. . . in deciding which objectives you will teach and which you will not teach to which students . . .	4. *Decision, and brings back the teaching practice in a general way*
. . . to have a high likelihood that each student learns the objectives selected for him or her?	5. *Student impact*

Curriculum Example	*Question Elements*
When developing units of study around the district curriculum objectives . . .	1. *Condition and situation*
. . . AND thinking about using a thematic approach to the teaching of these objectives . . .	2. *Teacher reflection on curricular or instructional teaching practice*

Curriculum Example	Question Elements
. . . what thoughts go on in your mind . . .	3. *Choice*
. . . about which themes to select . . .	4. *Decision, and brings back the teaching practice in a general way*
. . . to impact student understanding of the objectives?	5. *Student impact*

Instructional Example	Question Elements
When you are planning your assessments on your lesson objectives . . .	1. *Situation*
. . . AND thinking about the ways you will assess learning as well as how you will use the data . . .	2. *Teacher reflection on curricular or instructional teaching practice*
. . . what thoughts go on in your mind . . .	3. *Choice*
. . . in determining the assessments you will administer and the use of the data . . .	4. *Decision, and brings back the teaching practice in a general way*
. . . to help each student achieve that which you wish him or her to learn?	5. *Student impact*

Instructional Example	Question Elements
When you are delivering your lessons around the district curriculum and are posing questions around the critical attributes of the objectives . . .	1. *Situation and condition*
. . . AND thinking about the variety of ways you could have students respond . . .	2. *Teacher reflection on curricular or instructional teaching practice*

(Continued)

(Continued)

Instructional Example	Question Elements
. . . what criteria do you use . . .	3. *Choice*
. . . to decide which type of "student response approach" you will use . . .	4. *Decision, and brings back the teaching practice in a general way*
. . . to help each student learn the attributes of the objectives?	5. *Student impact*

Instructional Example	Question Elements
When planning your units around the district curriculum . . .	1. *Situation (and possible condition)*
. . . AND thinking about the activities you might select . . .	2. *Teacher reflection on curricular or* instructional *teaching practice*
. . . what thoughts go on in your mind . . .	3. *Choice*
. . . about which of the activities to select from all the possible activities . . .	4. *Decision, and brings back the teaching practice in a general way*
. . . to have a high likelihood that each student learns the objectives?	5. *Student impact*

Before you state your reflective question, it is cardinal that you determine the curricular or instructional teaching practices that you might address. This is the one thing that you probably will want to note or have in your mind when you leave the teacher's room. This is doubly important if you think you might have a conversation with the teacher.

Once you have the teaching practice clearly in your mind, ask yourself when the teacher would typically make this decision—when planning, when teaching, and so on. This leads you to the first element of the reflective question. Although the teaching practice is the second part of the question, it is the first in importance. You should carefully consider the question before you ask it.

How You Think It—Plan for It	Order in Which You State It
1. Teacher reflection on curricular or instructional teaching practice	1. Situation (and possible condition)
2. Situation (and possible condition)	2. Teacher reflection on curricular or instructional teaching practice
3. Choice	3. Choice
4. Decision, and brings back the teaching practice in a general way	4. Decision, and brings back the teaching practice in a general way
5. Student impact	5. Student impact

Now it is time for you to try writing the phrases of a reflective question for each of the two teachers in the scenarios highlighted in Chapter 2. Take the teaching practice you have already selected and try writing the reflective question, listing each phrase in the order in which you would state it. The five elements are listed for you, though eventually you will have them memorized:

Five Elements of the Reflective Question	**Your Reflective Question For the Language Arts Teacher (Chapter 2)**
1. Situation (and possible condition)	
2. Teacher reflection on curricular or instructional teaching practice	
3. Choice	
4. Decision, and brings back the teaching practice in a general way	

(Continued)

(Continued)

Five Elements of the Reflective Question	Your Reflective Question For the Language Arts Teacher (Chapter 2)
5. *Student impact*	

Five Elements of the Reflective Question	Your Reflective Question For the Mathematics Teacher (Chapter 2)
1. *Situation (and possible condition)*	
2. *Teacher reflection on curricular or instructional teaching practice*	
3. *Choice*	
4. *Decision, and brings back the teaching practice in a general way*	
5. *Student impact*	

Now, practice this orally two or three times. It will take multiple practice opportunities to change the way you ask questions. The reflective question must be used in a conversation. By itself, out of context, the question might be easily misunderstood; however, within the context of a conversation it works quite well. Often it might take several sentences to present all the elements of the reflective question. It works best if stated in phrases with pauses, such as in the following example:

"I had an idea. I thought you might enjoy reflecting on questioning strategies. When you are planning lessons and thinking about questions and student responses you might use to help students in their learning, what criteria do you use to decide which questioning strategies you will use? And what criteria do you use to decide who to call on for students to achieve the objectives?"

We have found that when you are first starting to try out the reflective question, the most common errors are the following:

- The teaching behavior is not placed immediately after the situation. Rather, it is placed after the "what" in the set of phrases. This removes the positive presupposition that assumes the teacher does think about the teaching practice, and it often moves the teacher to a knowledge-level response.
- Failure to be clear about the teaching practice—the statement lacks precision and may be confusing to the teacher.
- Trying to put more than one teaching practice into the question.
- Using the past tense—you are probably talking about the lesson and not about teacher practices.
- Using a reflective question when you feel strongly about the answer. The teacher will not be fooled, and you will probably have moved backward in your relationship with him or her.

After you pose the question, it will be the teacher's choice whether he or she chooses to reflect on this question and whether he or she chooses to have a conversation with you about it.

There are several levels of questions. This chapter has presented the initial level. Its purpose is to bring to the teacher's awareness the decisions he or she makes during planning, as well as the thought processes (or criteria) behind the decisions. It is suggested that when you first attempt to state the "choice" element of a reflective question that you use the phrase, "What criteria do you use . . ."

THE REFLECTIVE CONVERSATION

Now let's examine the transactional medium in which the reflective question is embedded. The entire conversation provides the *context* for the reflective question. This is shown in Table 3.11.

Table 3.11 Conversation Attributes and Sequence for Collaborative-Interdependent With Reflective Inquiry

- Set time frame—three to four minutes.
- Make positive statement about reflection.
- Focus on curricular or instructional teaching practice that will be the focus on your reflective conversation.
- Indicate the teacher decision point observed during the classroom observation that triggered this area for reflection in your mind.
- *Pose reflective question.*
- Allow time for clarification and interaction on question, as needed.
- Exit quickly with an offer of further conversation later, if the teacher desires.

The following is an example of the coaching side of a conversation, which is collaborative—reflective and interactive.

Table 3.12 is an example of how the reflective, collaborative conversation might proceed (the coach's statements only), along with the attributes of the conversation.

Table 3.12 Example of Collaborative-Interdependent Reflective Conversation From Coach's Perspective With Attributes of Conversation (does not include teacher comments)

What the Coach Might Say	*Attributes*
Hi. Do you have about five minutes? I have been thinking about a reflective question you might value.	Set time frame.
I know you enjoy being analytical and reflective on your curricular and instructional decisions, and I have a curricular question that I think is interesting—and thought you might think so also.	Make positive statement about reflection.
The teaching practice is about the decisions you make regarding the integration of objectives into lessons and units of study across the disciplines.	Curricular or instructional teaching practice will be the focus of your reflective conversation.
What made me think about this was that in today's lesson you were having the students compose a written word problem around a mathematics problem, and you were expecting the students to write a paragraph, use correct grammatical structure, and set up the word problem so it would be easily understood by a reader.	Indicate the teacher decision point you observed during the classroom observation that triggered this area for reflection in your mind.

What the Coach Might Say	*Attributes*
It seemed to me that you were making a decision about the integration of objectives. And the idea I had was about the thought process you undertake in terms of selecting objectives and when to integrate and when not to.	
So, here is the question:	Pose reflective question.
• When you are planning your units of study around the district curriculum . . . • . . . and thinking about whether to integrate objectives or not . . . • . . . what criteria do you use . . . • . . . to decide when to use integration and with which objectives . . . • . . . in order to expedite the student learning opportunities around the objectives?	
[After the teacher talks a little, you might need to clarify the teaching practice.]	Allow time for clarification and interaction on question, as needed.
Well, I need to go. Let me know if you think this was a meaningful reflective question for you. And, if you want, find me later and we'll chat about your thoughts.	Exit quickly with an offer of further conversation later, if the teacher desires.

Now it is time for you to practice the reflective question within a conversation. Using the teaching practice for one of the statements you have already written, write out the conversation.

Practice on the Collaborative-Interdependent Reflective Conversation	
(Outline your comments in the left-hand column.)	
What You Might Say	**Attributes**
	Set time frame.
	Make positive statement about reflection.

(Continued)

(Continued)

Practice on the Collaborative-Interdependent Reflective Conversation	
(Outline your comments in the left-hand column.)	
What You Might Say	**Attributes**
	Curricular or instructional teaching practice will be the focus of your reflective conversation.
	Indicate the teacher decision point observed during the classroom observation that triggered this area for reflection in your mind.
	Pose reflective question.
	Allow time for clarification and interaction on question, as needed.
	Exit quickly with an offer of further conversation later, if the teacher desires.

CAUTIONS IN USING THE REFLECTIVE QUESTION AND CONVERSATION

There are a few cautions about the reflective question and the conversation that need to be stated. The conversation around the teaching practice is to be professional and neutral. Make positive statements about the person's reflections, but exclude judgmental words about the practice itself.

How you begin to use this particular walk-through and reflective approach is critical. Teachers must be an integral part of the decision to move in this direction. Time spent in preparing a culture of reflection is imperative if it has been lacking. An entire chapter in this book is devoted to setting the stage for the use of the reflective-inquiry approach proposed in this chapter. This approach requires trust between the principal and the teachers and also enhances that trust when used appropriately. This approach will backfire if it seems that you are interrogating teachers or that you are being accusatory.

If you find the teacher shifting to a defensive posture, insert in your statement a reminder regarding the type of conversation you wish this to be—a professional, nonjudgmental conversation that is to be interactive and thought-provoking in nature. You might say something like, "It sounds like you think I want a particular answer to my question. I don't. The answer lies within you, not me. Remember, I don't even need a response from you. It's okay. It's your choice as to whether you want to think about this question further and whether or not you wish to discuss it with me."

The reflective question is a gift. It's planting a seed for future growth. Its purpose is to enhance a person's thinking on the journey and quest to learn about how he or she makes particular decisions and choices. It is not about answering to a supervisor. Because so many staff members are familiar with a hierarchical approach to supervision and are familiar with the dictum, "Give the right answer," we have to assist them in their understanding of this major shift to adult-adult professional collaboration.

Over time, teachers will begin to give us reflective questions about our work and help us grow in our practice. The goal is, eventually, to foster mutual professional interactions as well as increased self-analysis in our professional discourse.

The toughest challenge with this type of reflection, however, has to do with supervisors—our thinking and past habits. We are so used to being direct that we may find it difficult to use a different approach to professional inquiry. Some who have had difficulty with this new approach think that the reflective question is wishy-washy. But upon further investigation, we have found that these are the individuals who simply really want to tell the teacher how to behave and what to do. It has also been our experience that using direct statements with experienced teachers seldom changes their behavior, and that it even tends to alienate them.

We need to ask ourselves why we would continue to use such a style. Because it makes us feel good? We get something off our chest? A person who uses such an approach is not the type of supervisor we would like to see in the field. We do not want to be inspectors or "fix-it" people. However, most of us have been trained to do just that—judge and tell people what to do. It's the old foreman model left over from the factory. It's outdated.

We are about providing the basis for professional adults to work together beneficially and successfully. Our goal is to learn together. It's not about teachers answering to the authority of the principal. Rather, it is about creating a community of learners.

The following table illustrates the shift in thinking we are advocating by using our reflective-inquiry approach with staff.

Traditional	*Transformational*
Controlling environment	Growth environment
Hierarchical structure	Community of learners
Rewards, bribes, and punishments	Recognition for growth
Extrinsic motivation	Intrinsic motivation
Supervisor control	Inner locus of control
Origin of behaviors—Others	Origin of behavior—Self
Boss manager	Lead manager
Work as task	Work as joy
Approval	Increase capacity
Need others for efficacy	Self-efficacy

This chapter has provided details about follow-up conversations to our walk-through approach. The three types of approaches exist on a continuum from direct to indirect and are illustrated below. When we are at one end of the continuum—the direct—we are using more of a behaviorist approach to coaching teachers. As we move to the interactive, collaborative mode, we are using a constructivist approach to our work (see Lambert et al., 1995). We are also moving from a comprehension level of cognition to an analytical level of cognition.

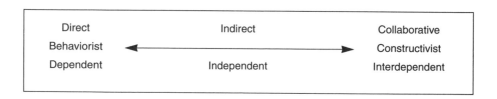

Think back to the start of this chapter and your thoughts about a differentiated dialogue. How has this chapter influenced your thoughts? Discuss with your learning partner or think about it yourself and respond in the space provided:

Current Reflections on the Direct Feedback, Indirect Reflection, and Collaborative Reflection Follow-Up Conversations

(Write your comments here.)

_____

_____

_____

_____

Constructing a Taxonomy of Reflective Questions and Their Use in the Classroom Walk-Through

Experience with the Downey Walk-Through model of classroom observation with its focus on the reflective question has indicated that both teachers and principals begin to move into an expanded and deeper form of interaction over time. As classroom experience is accrued, teachers become aware of many more dimensions of their work. The often subtle relationships between their own actions and reactions begin to be connected to student responses and the construction of classroom environmental learning opportunities, the use of manipulatives, and a broad range of differentiated learning activities. Figure 4.1 illustrates this relationship.

The level of collaboration shown in Figure 4.1 relates to work with a principal who is enabling the teacher to become more autonomous, interdependent, and highly competent in the classroom via the increasing depth of the reflective questions in use. While the principal will want to select reflective questions that promote increased reflection and possible growth, he or she will not want to employ questions that are perceived as

Figure 4.1   The Relationship Between Classroom Experience and the Depth of Reflective Questions

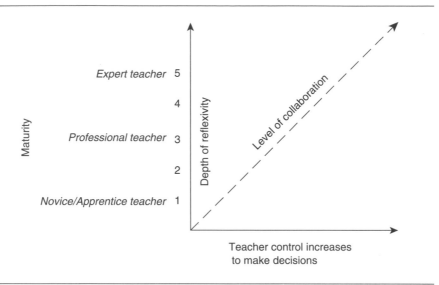

Figure 4.2   A Model for the Framing of a Reflective Question—The Creation of Cognitive Dissonance

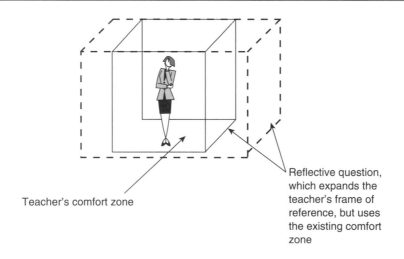

too difficult or even "too theoretical" for a teacher to handle. The reflective question posed to the beginning teacher should not be the same as one posed to an experienced teacher. The purpose of the reflective question is not to stump the teacher; it should be within the range of the teacher's competencies and interest. It should be partially in and partially out of the teacher's comfort zone, as shown in Figure 4.2.

A reflective question should entail two dimensions. First, the question should be anchored in the teacher's current comfort zone and professional repertoire. Second, the question should move the teacher out of his or her comfort zone into an expanded context. Part of this conversation should involve the creation of *cognitive dissonance*. Such dissonance refers to disjointedness between the teacher's current repertoire and an expanded context in which the repertoire offers room for professional development. This gap cannot be too large or it becomes disabling. The "art" of the reflective question involves the principal knowing (sometimes by trying) how much dissonance a teacher can handle. It should be enough to cause some discomfort in a positive way, and hence promote intellectual/conceptual/cognitive growth, but not so much as to be overwhelming. Provoking a response to an overwhelming scenario could seem like punishment.

Creating a reflective question involves construction of a query that has no single "correct" answer and that leads to a conversation about more general teaching practices. A reflective question's components of the "situation" and "curricular or instructional teaching practice," when presented as positive presuppositions, provide for the first dimension, that of the comfort zone of the teacher. The second dimension, that of extension of the zone of comfort, occurs in the "choice" and "decision" elements of the reflective question. This is illustrated in Figure 4.3.

Figure 4.3   The Root and the Extension in Framing the Reflective Question

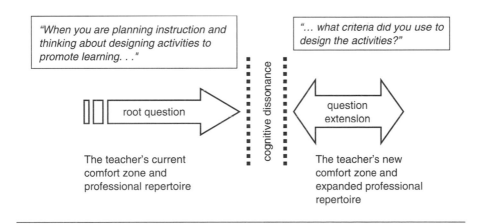

THE NOVICE/APPRENTICE

Comfort Zone Question Root: "When you are planning your math lessons (situation) and thinking about the type of problems you might select (teaching practice) *(Extension—moving the teacher out of the comfort zone slightly)* what factors do you use (choice) to decide on the selection of problems (decision) to move students forward in their learning (student impact)?"

In the conversation in which the reflective question takes place, the principal introduces the teaching practice and starts with a concrete, observed instance where the novice/apprentice teacher was working in order to bring awareness to the teacher of the current practice (comfort zone), and then *extends* the awareness zone slightly through the teaching of extended information. In the conversation, the teacher may even say something like, "You know, I just used the examples in the book; I didn't even think about the kinds of student responses I might get." The reflective question then evolves throughout the conversation and is posed near the close of the conversation. Remember, a more direct approach is used with the neophyte teacher initially, during which we are to teach about the teaching practice.

THE PROFESSIONAL TEACHER

Comfort Zone Question Root: "After you plan your lesson activities in social studies and use your criteria for designing those activities *(Extension— moving the senior teacher out of the comfort zone)*, what thoughts go on in your mind as you are using activities to help you determine if what is transpiring in the classroom is congruent with your plans, in order that your activities enhance student learning?"

In this example, the principal knows from interactions and repeated observations of this senior teacher that the teacher uses various criteria to select learning activities. The question is aimed at the idea of *fidelity of design,* that is, whether or not the criteria the teacher has selected are carried through. It doesn't matter at this point if they are or aren't. What matters is bringing the process to the consciousness of the teacher's classroom repertoire so the teacher is aware of the idea of congruence between setting up activities and using data to determine if the activities were congruent with the design criteria. Connecting these issues is the principal's goal.

THE EXPERT TEACHER

Comfort Zone Question Root: "When you are working on different dimensions of a current issue using small-group work and thinking about strategies you might use to differentiate instruction so that each student learns the content from each of the group's efforts, what criteria do you

Figure 4.4   The Stance of the Principal With the Reflective Question in a
Collegial Interaction With a Neophyte, Senior, or Expert Teacher

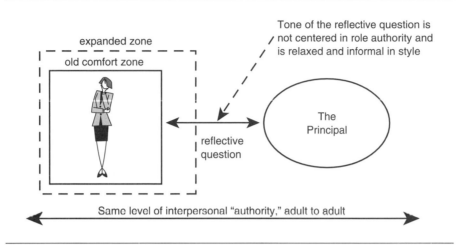

use to select those strategies that will help each student master the desired learnings?"

In this interaction, the principal is having a conversation with a very experienced and expert teacher. This is a teacher who has already mastered most of the classroom mechanics and has demonstrated that he or she can break out multiple activities from sets of goals and objectives. The principal's observation reveals that, as expected, students are participating differentially. This is not necessarily a detriment, but needs to be accommodated since students may be involved in different activities in different ways. In the give and take of group dynamics, participation may vary. Yet, even while this fact of group interaction will be present, the principal is interested in knowing how this expert teacher is ensuring that all of the learning comes together at some point for each student and in knowing how the teacher knows. The principal expects the teacher to know and isn't fishing for a "gotcha"; rather, the principal is using the question as a starting point for reflection and a possible future collaborative conversation. The collegial aspect of interaction is often communicated by the tone and personal dynamics used between the principal and teacher. The tone of voice used by the principal cannot be that of an authoritarian adult to a child. The tone used should be that of a friend to a friend, as between partners, each of whom is respectful of the other. This relationship is shown in Figure 4.4.

When thinking about the curricular or instructional practice you might bring to the teacher in the form of a reflective question, you need to know the teacher well and keep in mind the following criteria. The content of the reflective question should be

- At the right level of difficulty for the teacher—partially in the comfort zone and partially in the expanded zone.
- Seen as meaningful and of value to the teacher.
- Tied to a current interest of the teacher.
- Geared toward the readiness of the teacher.
- Related to the school- or district-improvement focus.
- Potentially impacting student achievement.
- Reflective of the relationship between the supervisor and the teacher.
- Tied to past reflective questions posed.

The priority of these criteria may be different for different teachers. Here is a reflective question that models this approach:

Situation: When you are in a classroom observing a teacher and thinking that today would be a good time to present a reflective question . . .

Response: . . . and thinking about which of the many curricular or instructional teaching practices you might pose . . .

Criteria: . . . what criteria do you use . . .

Decision: . . . to decide on one particular practice over another . . .

Impact: . . . in order to stretch the teacher professionally in his or her self-analysis of practices?

Figure 4.5 maps the levels of complexity of the questions that may arise in the Downey curriculum walk-through. Level 1 presents a range of possible reflective questions regarding the selection of criteria for planning the curriculum content and instructional activities to be employed in the classroom. This level relates to any event in the classroom in which students may encounter curriculum content; for example, as students receive directions from the teacher, at a computer center, in learning centers, and so on. The question at this level could also relate to the nature of independent study and homework completed.

A Level 2 reflective question relates to the fidelity of the teacher's decisions in using the criteria. The question posed incorporates the idea of how a teacher determines if his or her decisions consistently use the criteria the teacher thinks he or she is using. We want the teachers to think about remaining faithful to the criteria that they think they are using.

Level 3 moves the teachers from thinking about the design of their decisions to whether the decisions are getting the results desired. The reflective question asks the teacher to think about those factors he or she is using to determine the effectiveness of the criteria the teacher is using to make decisions. Is the teacher getting the results desired?

Figure 4.5   Mapping the Dimensions of Complexity in an Elementary School
Classroom

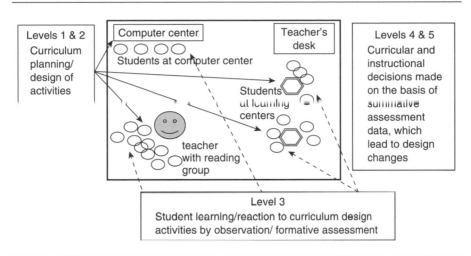

Level 3 reflective questions pertain to the use of formative or ongoing observation and assessment. At this level, reflective questions would pertain to judgments by the teacher regarding student reactions and interactions with the teacher and with other students. The database used by teachers at this stage would consist mostly of immediate responses, perhaps with some weekly or even semimonthly assessments. But the database would not consist of yearly accountability assessments conducted by the state.

Level 4 relates to the summative type of assessment represented in formal, paper-and-pencil tests that make up state or some national assessments. The data from these sorts of assessments represent longer stretches of learning that have occurred in the classroom. Such data may form the basis for changes in the selection of curriculum content (to attain improved alignment, for example), in the design of learning centers and activities to more closely connect with the content and reinforce the necessary learning, and in the criteria the teacher uses to judge formative feedback.

In the final level, Level 5, a reflective question is posed to help the teacher think about whether he or she has reached the best results he or she is going to obtain with the current set of criteria and decisions. It helps the teacher feel confident that this particular curricular or instructional practice is working at its optimum level. The question for the teacher focuses on that point in his or her thinking where a teacher believes that his or her curricular and instructional decisions about a given practice are maximizing student learning.

These levels can be conceptualized as the teacher selecting curriculum content based on some kind of criteria for selection of that content.

This decision is followed by the design of the classroom environment as it pertains to student learning stations and student activities. As the teacher plans and carries out the decision, the teacher notes whether he or she is using the criteria in a reliable way throughout his or her practice. Next, as the teacher is teaching, he or she is beginning to note whether the decisions made are working. Further, as the teacher implements these decisions, he or she begins to receive feedback from students. Observations reveal if the selection of the content was appropriate and if it was presented or taught in ways that led to differentiated instruction so that all children could attain success. This involves the kind of summative assessment that leads to an appraisal of a more grand design and scope. The range of data involved may lead to sweeping changes in classroom environments, revised selection of learning activities and learning centers, and modes of presentation based on learner responses and learning styles. Finally, the teacher determines whether or not the criteria being used and the decisions being made regarding a particular curricular or instructional practice are getting maximum results in student learning.

An expert teacher usually exhibits a near mastery of these interactions and can easily adjust classroom dynamics based on formative assessments. Since formal, state-imposed assessments are still relatively new, even expert teachers may not fully understand the deep impact of state testing on the grand design of classroom instruction. Some state assessments will rigidify classroom interactions, leading to direct methods of instruction that improve test scores but which in the longer term may be deadly to learner curiosity and the desire to learn that which is not tested. Teachers and their principals will constantly have to balance the demands for accountability and improved test scores with the effects these instruments have on the affective domain, which is so crucial to learner motivation. This balancing act can certainly be part of the reflective dialogue embedded in a reflective question between teachers and principals. Much of the "answer" will depend on local context and the penalties and rewards involved.

A "Taxonomy of Reflective Questions" is shown in Table 4.1. After the principal determines what kinds of questions will promote reflection and an expanded repertoire of teacher work, the taxonomy can be used to frame the questions.

Table 4.2 is an example of how these levels of questions might sound regarding the instructional practice of selecting activities to use in lessons.

Table 4.3 is an example of how these levels of questions might sound regarding the curricular practice of integration of objectives in lessons.

Table 4.1   Taxonomy of Reflective Questions: Components and Starter Phrases

Reflective Question Components

Components	Level 1	Level 2	Level 3	Level 4	Level 5
	What is your knowledge and what is the priority of criteria you use in making decisions? (Design)	Do your decisions meet the criteria you are using? (Design)	Are the decisions you are making using your criteria getting the desired results? (Design and Delivery)	How do you use student learning results (observed or measured) to inform your use of the criteria in the future? (Design and Delivery)	How do you know if you have reached the best student achievement results you are going to obtain with your criteria? (Design and Delivery)
Situation/ Condition	When planning, teaching,	When planning, carrying out your planning	When teaching	When you are assessing the results of your planning regarding	When you are reflecting about your planning and teaching
Teacher Action and Teaching Practice	And thinking about the . . .	And thinking about the consistent use of your criteria for . . .	And thinking about whether you are getting the desired results from the criteria you are using when you are planning regarding a practice	And thinking about how you might use the student assessment data to help determine whether your criteria might need modification	And thinking about whether your criteria result in maximum student achievement

(Continued)

Table 4.1 (Continued)

Components	Level 1	Level 2	Level 3	Level 4	Level 5
Choice	What criteria do you use and the priority of those criteria	What thoughts go on in your mind	What thoughts go on in your mind	What factors do you consider	What factors do you consider
Decision (mention teaching practice generally stated)	In deciding how to . . .	Regarding consistent use of your criteria on . . .	Regarding the usefulness of your criteria in getting the desired results from . . .	In deciding about the need for criteria modification for . . .	To decide if the criteria and their use are at their optimum level for you
Student Impact	In helping each student achieve the learnings you desire?	In helping each student achieve the learnings you desire?	In helping each student achieve the learnings you desire?	In helping each student achieve the learnings you desire?	In helping each student achieve the learnings you desire?

92

Table 4.2 Reflective Question Examples by the Five Levels: Instructional Practice Example

Components	Level 1	Level 2	Level 3	Level 4	Level 5
	What is your knowledge and priority of criteria you use in making decisions? *(Design)*	Do your decisions meet the criteria you are using? *(Design)*	Are the decisions you are making using your criteria getting the desired results? *(Design and Delivery)*	How do you use student learning results (observed or measured) to inform your use of the criteria in the future? *(Design and Delivery)*	How do you know if you have reached the best student achievement results you are going to obtain with your criteria? *(Design and Delivery)*
Situation/ Condition	When you are planning your science lessons around the varying levels of student achievement	When you are planning your science lessons around the varying levels of student achievement	When you are teaching your science lessons around the varying levels of student achievement	When you are assessing the results of your planning and teaching of the science lessons around the varying levels of student achievement	When you are reflecting about your planning and teaching of your science lessons around the varying levels of student achievement
Teacher Action and Teaching Practice	And thinking about the selection of activities for the lessons,	And thinking about the consistent use of your criteria for selection of activities,	And thinking about whether you are getting the desired results from the criteria you are using when you are planning the activity selection,	And thinking about how you might use the student assessment data to help determine whether your criteria might need modification in selecting activities,	And thinking about whether your criteria result in maximum student achievement,

(Continued)

Table 4.2 (Continued)

Components	Level 1	Level 2	Level 3	Level 4	Level 5
Choice	What criteria do you use and what is the priority of those criteria	What thoughts go on in your mind	What thoughts go on in your mind	What factors do you consider	What factors do you consider
Decision (mention teaching practice generally stated)	To decide on those activities	Regarding consistent use of your criteria on activity selection decisions	Regarding the usefulness of your criteria in getting the desired results from the activities selected	In deciding about the need for criteria modification for selection of activities	To decide whether the criteria and your use of them is at the optimum level for you
Student Impact	That will help each student achieve the learnings you desire?	In helping each student achieve the learnings you desire?	In helping each student achieve the learnings you desire?	That will help each student achieve the learnings you desire?	In helping each student achieve the learning you desire?

Table 4.3 Reflective Question Examples by the Five Levels: Curricular Practice Example

Components	Level 1	Level 2	Level 3	Level 4	Level 5
	What is your knowledge and what is the priority of the criteria you use in making decisions? (*Design*)	Do your decisions meet the criteria you are using? (*Design*)	Are the decisions you are making using your criteria getting the desired results? (*Design and Delivery*)	How do you use student learning results (observed or measured) to inform your use of the criteria in the future? (*Design and Delivery*)	How do you know if you have reached the best student achievement results you are going to obtain with your criteria? (*Design and Delivery*)
Situation/ Condition	When you are planning your units of study around the district curriculum	When you are planning your units of study around the district curriculum	When you are teaching your units of study around the district curriculum	When you are assessing the results of planning your units of study around the district curriculum	When you are reflecting about planning and teaching your units of study around the district curriculum
Teacher Action and Teaching Practice	And thinking about the possible integration of objectives—when to integrate and which objectives to integrate	And thinking about the consistent use of your criteria for determining which objective you will integrate objectives, if any	And thinking about whether you are getting the desired results from the criteria you are using when you are planning for the integration of objectives	And thinking about how you might use the student assessment data to help determine whether your criteria might need modification for the integration of objectives	And thinking about whether your criteria for your decisions regarding the integration of objectives results in maximum student achievement

(Continued)

Table 4.3 (Continued)

Components	Level 1	Level 2	Level 3	Level 4	Level 5
Choice	What criteria do you use and what is the priority of those criteria	What thoughts go on in your mind	What thoughts go on in your mind	What factors do you consider	What factors do you consider
Decision (mention teaching practice generally stated)	To decide on when to integrate and with which objectives	Regarding the consistent use of your criteria on integration decisions	Regarding the usefulness of your criteria in getting the desired results from the integration of objectives	In deciding about the need for criteria modification for integration of objectives	To decide whether the integration criteria and their use are at their optimum level for you
Student Impact	In helping each student achieve the learnings you desire?	In helping each student achieve the learnings you desire?	In helping each student achieve the learnings you desire?	In helping each student achieve the learnings you desire?	In helping each student achieve the learnings you desire?

The taxonomy is useful in expanding the way the principal views classroom dynamics. It is a kind of observational rubric that can be shared with teachers as well. It will serve to demystify what the principal is looking for when entering the classroom.

LIMITATIONS OF THE TAXONOMY

The taxonomy presented in this chapter is situated within the mainstream accountability movement that is so dominant at the present time in American education. The taxonomy "fits" this movement because it is based on the familiar input-process-output model that is behind how we think about making decisions and choices, observing their effects, and engaging in changes if things are not going as we would want or require in classrooms and schools. There may be other models for framing questions for classroom practice that are not centered on the input-process-output fulcrum, models in which the teacher is not envisioned as an "input" or "process," and where the "effects" are not required to lead to test scores or other kinds of "products" as "outcomes."

Accountability schemes require simple models that are predicated on obvious "cause-effect" relationships. Real life and learning often cannot be so simply equated. One thinks of higher order conceptual thinking where, after preliminary instruction, the learner assumes the role of teacher and engages in the kind of innovative or path breaking work that occurs in scientific research; creative and interpretive art forms such as painting or sculpture; and various forms of creative writing, poetry, and/or musical composition.

An underlying assumption about the use of the taxonomy, whether the input-process-output variety or some other type of contemplative rubric, is that its purpose is to enhance the competence, range of awareness, autonomy, and independence of the classroom teacher. The position of the teacher as a fully functioning, autonomous professional remains the cornerstone of the purpose of the reflective question.

Establishing Logistical Procedures for Implementing the Walk-Through Process

Now that you have a basic understanding of the walk-through process, it is time to turn your attention to how you might use this process in your own school.

FINDING THE TIME

One of the first considerations to think about is finding the time necessary to conduct walk-throughs. Even though these are short, 2- to 3-minute visits to classrooms, it is important to develop a schedule for conducting them. It is also important to make use of the unscheduled moments in your day. This is not hard to do since the visits are short. We know from research that most principals spend from 40 to 80 percent of their time in or around the office area. An additional 23 to 40 percent is spent in hallways and on the playground. About 11 percent is spent off campus, and only about 2.5 to 10 percent is spent in classrooms. Yet, the advantage of observing the work of teachers and students in classrooms, of problem solving with teachers regarding curriculum and instruction, and of facilitating teacher reflection can significantly impact student achievement.

Form 5.1   Current Classroom Walk-Through Time

Time of Day	Time in Minutes					
	Mon.	Tues.	Wed.	Thurs.	Fri.	Total
Before school day						
Morning						
Lunch						
Afternoon						
After school						
Total						

Take a few minutes now to think about the time you currently spend in classrooms or engaging in reflective dialogue with teachers and jot that down on a form like the one shown above. Do this by reflecting on a typical week.

Add up the totals both for day of the week and for time of day, and determine the present amount of time you are currently spending conducting walk-throughs. Now, think about your week and develop a new walk-through schedule using a form like the one shown in Form 5.2. Think about the before-school and afterschool time as an appropriate time to engage in reflective dialogue. These conversations can also be held during a teacher's planning time. Remember, you will not be engaging in reflective dialogue with each teacher, but this time needs to be built into your schedule. Even though this activity asks you to specify a walk-through schedule for a week, in reality you should implement this process so that you are not following the same schedule each day. Teachers become aware of your walk-through patterns very quickly. They need to become comfortable with the fact that you might visit their classrooms at any time on any day. While there is no magic formula for the amount of time you should spend conducting walk-throughs, a guideline some principals use is 25 percent of their time per day. If you are working an eight-hour day, this translates into two hours per day. Of course, you want to get into all of your teachers' classrooms as often as possible. Depending on the size of your building, you may want to consider encouraging additional staff to get training in this process. The process seems to work best when both principals and assistant principals are trained. This enables them to conduct both team and individual walk-throughs. Many of the districts utilizing this process have also now trained department chairs, mentor teachers, and central office staff.

Analyze the difference between the time you are spending conducting walk-throughs now and the time you want to spend. Now think about the

Form 5.2   Proposed Classroom Walk-Through Time

Time of Day	Time in Minutes					
	Mon.	Tues.	Wed.	Thurs.	Fri.	Total
Before school day						
Morning						
Lunch						
Afternoon						
After school						
Total						

activities you are currently engaged in that you can either eliminate or spend less time doing. Implementing these changes will require the support of central administration as well as the setting of new expectations for teachers, staff, and parents regarding your availability. Walk-throughs must become one of the highest priorities in your daily activities.

In addition to a formal schedule for conducting walk-throughs, don't forget about times when you have a few minutes and could incorporate an unplanned walk-through into your schedule. For instance, if an appointment is cancelled, use that time for walk-throughs. If you are checking on a physical plant problem somewhere in the building, conduct a walk-through on your way to inspect the problem and another on your way back. Some principals do not enter the building by the front door when they return from an outside meeting. Rather, they enter by a side door or at the back of the building and work their way to the office by conducting a few walk-throughs on the way. We recently learned of a principal who programmed his screen saver to periodically flash *Walk-Through, Walk-Through* as a reminder to get out from behind the desk and visit classrooms.

PREPARING STAFF, STUDENTS, AND PARENTS

It is important that staff, students, and parents all be made aware of this new technique you are going to be using to support the continued development of the leaning environment in the school. It would be a mistake to simply begin using the Downey Walk-Through process without talking to teachers about what you are doing. Yes, they are accustomed to having you in their classrooms, but many times when the principal enters the classroom, everything stops. The teacher directs the students' attention to the principal and often the students, particularly at the elementary level, stop what they are doing and say something like, "Good morning, Mr. Jones." Or, the teacher will stop what she is doing and ask the principal, "May I help you?" or "Did you want to talk to me?" Also, it is obvious that you are "looking with a focus" and occasionally jotting down notes on a card or on your organizer. Without the proper orientation, you can rest assured that you will receive a call from the building union representative before the end of the day unless this orientation has taken place.

The teacher orientation can take many routes. Some principals use all of the suggestions we include in this chapter. First, it is important that you inform your staff that you are trying out a new technique to enhance the reflective dialogues about instruction that take place in the school. You are taking the lead in using this technique, the goal of which is to improve student achievement. Most principals provide staff with an overview of the process at a staff meeting. If you attend formal training for the Downey Walk-Through, you will receive a computer presentation that you can modify and adjust for your own purposes. In addition, many principals have combined both sending a memo to the staff and discussing the process at a faculty meeting. A sample memo follows for your consideration and modification.

As you know, I have just finished a seminar on reflective practice and on how to use the walk-through as a vehicle for reflective conversations. I wanted to pass on some helpful information about the content of the seminar. The purpose of the seminar was to provide administrators and others who coach teachers with several approaches for how to use a brief walk-through to create opportunities for meaningful reflective dialogue with staff. I will share this five-step observation structure with you in our next faculty meeting. I think you will be very pleased with it and may even want to begin using it as you walk into each other's classrooms. The walk-through technique will help us focus on the curriculum standards and objectives and also on the decisions teachers are making. Let me stress that these walk-throughs are non-evaluative in nature.

The focus of the seminar was on coaches visiting a classroom for a very short period of time in order to determine the objectives being taught and to think about possible reflective questions that could be posed to stretch teachers professionally. A reflective question is posed to teachers who are conscientious and who are eager to learn. The ultimate goal is to have all staff become self-reflective, self-analytical individuals who are always seeking increased efficiencies in order to help students learn. Further, another central goal is to encourage us to have collaborative dialogue about our work.

It is not expected that reflective questions be answered; rather, teachers should view the questions as tools that encourage them to seek out more knowledge. Teachers should be inspired to seek answer for themselves. Here is a sample reflective question on using prior learnings:

Situation:	*When you are planning your lessons around the district curriculum,*
Teaching Practice:	*and thinking about if and how you might use prior learnings in helping students with new learnings,*
Choice:	*what criteria do you use*
Decision:	*to decide about the use of prior learnings*
Student Impact:	*in helping students in their achievement of the new learnings?*

The questions are to be analytical in nature and meaningful. I hope to begin our journey in using reflective questions by asking them of myself in my work and sharing them with you. Further, I hope to use some in our faculty meetings so you can get acquainted with what we have learned. I think you will like these ideas as much as I did.

In this sample memo, reference is made to both the five-step observation process and the reflective dialogue. Some principals have chosen to introduce the five step process first and then provide information about the reflective dialogue at a later time. The decision is clearly up to you.

It is also important to bring the union on board before you begin using the technique. Meeting with union representatives individually or in groups, sharing this book with them, or encouraging them to go through the training are all ways of gaining their support.

It goes without saying that implementing this process requires a climate of trust between teachers and the principal. Certainly walk-throughs can be viewed negatively if the principal has not made the school environment a safe place for continued growth. The credibility of the building principal engaged in this process is critical. This process has worked especially well for principals assuming responsibility for a new school, for first-time principals, and for principals who have established that trusting relationship with teachers. Only you can assess where you are in relation to these examples. If you are not certain the trust level is there, you might want to consider starting the process with teacher volunteers who are willing to work with you as you become more proficient with the walk-through, or you may want to begin by working with your new hires. Newly hired teachers are very receptive to this type of dialogue. With new hires, the principal is able to establish an expectation for "how things are" in his or her school environment. Most districts are hiring about 5 to 10 percent new staff each year. Over a three-year period, this amounts to 15 to 30 percent of the faculty. And by combining new hires with volunteers, the majority of the teachers in the building will be involved in the process of reflective dialogue in a short period of time.

As mentioned before, teachers need to know that when you enter the room, you do not want instruction to stop. There is no need for them to stop and explain to you what has happened before and what is going to happen next. They also need to know that it is okay if they are in a transition point in the lesson. It is not unusual for a principal to enter a classroom, see that a transition is under way and exit without staying the two to three minutes, only to return later after instruction is under way. Some principals like to conduct walk-throughs at the beginning of the day, others at the end of the day and during transitions. There is no right or wrong time to make classroom visits. The visits are not for making judgments about what is good or bad. Rather, their purpose is to engage in reflective dialogue about improving curriculum and instruction so that more students are learning at ever higher levels.

Students require little orientation to this walk-through technique. The teacher might want to let them know that the principal may enter the room at any time, and if so, that they are not to stop what they are doing to ask the principal a question or say "Hi." Rather, the principal is there to view the learning that is going on. Stories from secondary principals implementing this process are legion about them doing walk-throughs only to have the students later ask the teacher, "Who was that person?" That kind of question should become a thing of the past with the implementation of the Downey Walk-Through process.

Parents will need to know why you may not be immediately available to them when they call. They need to know that you are out and about in the building, engaged in improving the learning process with teachers. Actually, principals using this process are far more informed about what is actually happening in classrooms. They are often so aware of the instructional strategies teachers are using that they can provide parents with answers to questions without having to check with a specific classroom teacher. When such situations occur, parents are usually very impressed with the detailed knowledge the principal has about instruction in his or her building. When you are out of the office, parents may simply need to be assured about what you are doing when you are in classrooms. They also need to be supportive of the time you spend in the classrooms and with reflective dialogue after these visits. Parents can gain information about the walk-through process from your presentations at parent meetings, articles included in school newsletters, and through conversations with the executive committee of the parent organization.

RECORD KEEPING

The most important thing to remember about record keeping with this process is *Keep It Simple!* As you learned in Chapter 2, while you are in the classroom, you make notes about specifics related to the five steps. These notes are only for you. They do not go into anyone's personnel file. They are simply notes to jog your memory about what you saw. When we train principals in this process, we encourage them to use blank 3×5 index cards to record information. An example of the type of information recorded on these cards is outlined below.

Example of Information to Record During Classroom Visit

Name here	**Assignments here**
Date/time	
Curriculum here	**Instruction here**
Content	**Two or three decisions**
Context	
Cognition type	**Key** Circle topic if you plan to hold a conversation Box topic if you leave a note Check topic if you plan to watch
District Check	

Very soon after learning this process, many principals become so familiar with the system that they no longer even need to write. *Under no circumstances should checklists be used!* As stated earlier, checklists narrow the scope of vision for observing classrooms. You want to write down only those most important things that will enable you to see patterns over time and help you to home in on topics for a reflective dialogue that will be a meaningful growth opportunity for the teacher. Of course, it is important to note the name of the teacher, date, time of day, and subject/grade. This information enables you to be sure that you visit a classroom at a variety of times in the day and also shows you the frequency of your visits. Some principals start the week with a card for every teacher in the building. At the end of the week, all the cards should be used. Others record multiple visits to the same teacher on a single card. In the beginning, you may want to use a separate card for each visit and then later modify your record keeping to meet your needs.

Note the key on the example. If you planned to engage in a reflective dialogue with the teacher, you would circle the curricular decision point or the teaching practice. If you plan to leave a note, you can put a square around "note." If you have identified a potential pattern or trend you want to track over time, you may want to put a check mark next to that.

You will quickly develop a record-keeping system that makes sense to you and that enables you to record enough information but not too much. If teachers want to see what you are recording, show it to them. In fact, in the orientation sessions with faculty, you may want to show them some examples and explain what is on the card and why. The example below shows a card filled out.

Example One Way (3x5 card)

Mark Anders	**6th Grade**
8/19/01 11:35am	
Content	
• **Convert fractions to percent**	review strategies
• **Convert fractions to whole numbers**	real world/symbol.
• **Convert whole numbers to percent**	metacognition
Context	when/when not
• **symbolic**	
• **oral student response**	
Cognitive Type -K	
District Check: 4th	

(metacognition / when/when not are circled)

From the information on this card, we can see that the walk-through was done in a 6th-grade classroom during math class. The instructional objective dealt with converting fractions to percentages and whole numbers and converting whole numbers to percentages. These objectives were listed in the district curriculum at the 4th-grade level. Students were responding orally to symbolic problems. The instruction was at the knowledge level, using Bloom's Taxonomy. Teaching practices that could lead to reflective dialogue included review strategies, real-world versus symbolic problems, and metacognition (when and when not to use it). The principal decided to hold a reflective dialogue with this teacher about the teaching practice of metacognition. It is worth reinforcing that, when the principal is collecting these data, it is not with the intent of making judgments about decisions the teacher has made. It is about adults learning to improve practice.

Over time, principals develop their own unique recording practices. Remember to keep it simple. Limit the paperwork and the filing, and record just enough of what happened when you were in the room to use when having a follow-up conversation. When you exit the room, your note taking should be complete. Initially, you may have to consult the district curriculum guide to determine where the objectives are listed, but eventually you will become quite familiar with the written curriculum. We are finding that principals are becoming quite forceful in demanding that the district's written curriculum be in a format that is organized and specific enough to enable principals to easily use these documents with walk-throughs.

BOARD POLICY TO SUPPORT WALK-THROUGHS

Board policy can be helpful in supporting the implementation of the walk-through process. We recommend policies that direct the superintendent to develop procedures for implementing, monitoring, and assessing the effects of the walk-through process, including the follow-up reflective dialogue with teachers. These policies should also require the alignment of the written, taught, and tested curriculum; the utilization of effective, research-based instructional practices; and the periodic analysis of how effectively the process is being carried out. Finally, these policies should ensure that funds are provided for high-quality regular administrator training. The following is a partial list of topics that could be used for this training:

Curriculum Alignment

Deep Alignment

Curriculum Management

Data Disaggregation

Textbook/Resource/Student Artifact Calibration

Curriculum Monitoring

Reflective Conferences

Increasing Academic Learning Time

Effective Instructional Methods

School Planning for Change Interventions

Increasing Teacher and Student Engagement Rates

This approach is really about how principals employ coaching and collaboration in their work. It is a management and leadership strategy. While this book describes the walk-through process in some detail, to effectively implement it you should consider attending a formal training seminar. These training sessions are sponsored by Phi Delta Kappa (PDK) and Curriculum Management Systems, Inc. (CMSi).

Cultivating the Culture

Effectuating Change That Works

The aims and intentions of the walk-through coaching process developed by Carolyn Downey will probably resonate quite well with you, especially after you receive the introductory training or read the early chapters of this book. If you are like most of us, once you have acquired knowledge of this newfound process, your natural response will be to begin to use what you have learned. However, it's at this point that some of you may find the technique isn't working for you. Perhaps it just doesn't seem to work as well as it did in the training or as described in this book—but with patience and persistence, it will work and work well. What makes the difference? In this chapter, you will learn not only how to distinguish among factors that lead to success or failure, but also how to ease into implementation of the new paradigm or way of doing things, even if you have a challenging faculty situation.

The main purpose of this chapter is to explore experiences and narratives of practitioners who have tried the Downey walk-through with reflective follow-up conversations approach and who have largely been successful in "cultivating the culture." We then want to see what the practitioners have learned to do along the way and what they have learned *not* to do.

After reading through the lessons learned and experiences observed that are cited in this chapter, you should be able to do the following:

- Emulate and use the leadership steps necessary to successfully implement the five-step walk-through observation process and follow-up conversations without stumbling over obstacles to change.

- Recognize preconditions that need to be addressed before implementation.
- Take action to overcome the processes and practices that get in the way of effective walk-throughs and collaborative interactions, as well as tackle the issue of dealing with marginal teaching.
- Capitalize on the experiences of some practicing administrators who have successfully and effectively used the walk-through process.

LESSONS LEARNED ABOUT CHANGE IN EDUCATIONAL CULTURES

To begin, please ask yourself some simple questions:

1. What do I know about the process of change?

2. What helps people accept change and go along with a new way of doing things?

3. What do leaders have to do to bring about change?

4. How do I determine whether or not change is actually beneficial?

The process of change has been studied extensively over the past few decades, and some interesting and powerful notions about change have been revealed—some of which are far different than we had expected. For example, see the writings of Michael Fullan (2001) and others. Some of these important lessons learned are summarized below:

1. Change is possible. Given appropriate steps and commitments, successful change is possible. Moreover, things can be better despite our predilection to be complacent about our current conditions. The disenchantment facing those of us in PreK–12 schooling is well documented—one theory for change says "most of our schools are cold bureaucracies—not caring communities" (Wagner, 2001).

Given proper commitment, the walk-through observation can be effectively implemented, and teaching and learning can benefit accordingly (see Chapter 3 on research). The adage "if it ain't broke, don't fix it" no longer applies, at least in education. You must act—things in education have to get better if public credibility is to be sustained for the long term.

2. Leadership must initiate change. Change can occur without a leader's intervention or direction, but for effective and appropriate change to occur, leadership must make it happen. Random, chaotic change is less likely to get the results we need than systematic, deliberate activities that are either directed or supported by you as the leader. It is the major role of the leader to initiate change that is grounded in a valid and meaningful vision of educational efficacy.

3. Coerced change will probably fail. Coercive leadership or authoritarian leadership will effect a change, but the likelihood of the change persisting over time is low. In essence, change accomplished by the use of force (even when benevolent or well intentioned) or the judgmental imposition of change is not generally persistent or effective in the long run. More effective leadership styles are those that are democratic or affiliative (collaborative). The leader is the custodian of the vision, and it is the leader who focuses on the urgency and efficacy of successful learning for all. As Greenleaf (1996) said, "The leader leads well when leadership is, and is seen as, serving the dream and searching for a better one." Teachers *own* their own behavior and only *they* can change it.

4. Collaborative affiliations are crucial for successful change. In leading the change to using the walk-through process, you need to set aside your inspectorial demeanor and work collegially with your teachers. Teachers must perceive you as a colleague who is knowledgeable, interested in what they are doing, and worth the time it takes for reflective interactions. You can no longer be the boss, wielding top-down orders; you are more likely to succeed if you are the "helpful peer."

5. Slow change is better than rapid change (or, the tortoise is better than the hare). You are better off to move ahead *slooooowly* and with deliberation. We have learned that moving to the walk-through observations and the subsequent follow-up conversations over a lengthy period of time bolsters the likelihood for success in making change happen. Studies have shown that the protracted implementation of new processes fosters a more substantive chance of survival.

6. Change must make sense with follow-up conversation and solid, supportive evidence. You will find that "data-driven" approaches that usher in the walk-through process will lend greater credibility to what you're trying to do. Of course, data-driven information will include what you learn about how your teachers feel as you try to implement this new process and let them know that you are genuinely interested in helping them succeed, rather than "making book" or documenting evidence on what they do.

Principals are critical agents in the process of school change. They are the drivers and creators of school culture, and they need to acquire new skills to serve as effective agents of change rather than to act as mere conduits of externally mandated changes (Freedman & LaFleur, 2002). In order to make a positive impact on change or reform, principals (and other administrators) need to be more visible around their schools, know what is happening in classrooms, build and monitor the alignment of the written, taught, and measured curriculum, promote reflective practice, encourage public conversations about teaching and learning, support collaboration, articulate system and school vision, and be comfortable with creative tension and ambiguity (Freedman & LaFleur, 2002). If you are a principal, this may be a very different vision of what you thought you needed to do to *really* impact the quality of learning in your school.

In summary, change research has much to teach us about how to make the new paradigm of walk-through observations and reflective conversations work. Administrators must remember that truly effective change is painstakingly slow, broadly collaborative and collegial, supported by data and evidence, and led by a steadfast, affiliative leadership.

CHALLENGES AND BARRIERS TO CHANGE

Try as you will, no amount of dedication, commitment, or investment of time and energy will make the walk-through with collaborative, reflective inquiry process work in an adverse environment. Some preconditions definitely work against this constructive and supportive approach to enhancing learning. These preconditions in the school culture require your attention and action before moving ahead with the walk-through approach. The good news is that the follow-up conversation approach may be a big help to you in coping with these adverse school or organizational factors.

One key to your success will be found in the nature of your relationships with faculty and staff (Sergiovanni, 1999). Unless your current culture has some growth-producing elements, your best efforts could be stifled.

Given that many of our current educational practices are clearly inadequate, what is needed is a change in the underlying organizational structure of schools. Relationships that are built on a punitive system will suboptimize the walk-through process. Your presence in the classroom may be perceived as a threat, especially if your teachers know you only as an inspector or critic. If your teachers' image of you is one of a checklist-armed, stern-faced observer who supports them on successes but disparages them on shortcomings, you can't expect to make the switch easily to the role of a reflective helpmate. If your experience in observations has resembled the checklist-bearing inspector, initially you will need some time to rebuild a more positive, constructive relationship with your faculty. Teachers need to see you as a valuable resource for improving teaching and learning.

Teachers must know a great deal about student learning, motivation, and development to meet the needs of students who are unlikely to succeed on their own if they are not taught well in school (Darling-Hammond, 1990). That is where your role as a coach and mentor of teachers comes in. Your job in this new paradigm is to free the teachers' talent and skill through an effective and positive relationship that allows for reflective-questioning practices.

Some schoolwide procedures and operations can also suboptimize your best efforts to make the walk-through and follow-up process successful. A few examples of practices or problems that inhibit, if not subvert, constructive, reflective approaches include the following:

Ability grouping. Grouping students on the basis of ability has been categorically discarded as a useful practice for the augmentation of learning. Its destructive effects have been well documented by two decades of research (Educational Research Service, 1998) and legislation mandating inclusionary practices in public schooling. If tracking or ability grouping is operating in your school, it needs to be dealt with first. Although pedagogy sometimes includes it, we are pretending not to know what we know about learning if we support its continuance (Glickman, 1991). The walk-through process offers help to you here—using follow-up conversations about the impact of grouping is a very beneficial way to bring about change in this area.

Devastating dropout rates. If the clientele of your school are leaving in droves, all the wonderful pedagogy in the world won't help. The *raison d'etre* for the school isn't there. Heavy attrition rates are indicative of serious cultural problems, and until those are addressed and rectified, some other changes may have to wait. Again, group follow-up conversations about clientele attrition, using reliable data, can be an effective way to address this challenging issue.

Group ethnicity conflicts or failure. This is another vexatious issue that if present in your school needs to be placed high on the priority list of problems to be solved. John Dewey wrote that "what a community can do for the best of its children, it must do for all of its children" (Dewey, 1916/1944). Permitting some students to succeed while others fail means that the system is failing: The system must be fixed. Inequity and/or inequality of opportunity are cultural anomalies that cannot be tolerated in any educational institution.

Of course, this is not a complete list of institutional factors that you may need to tackle. There are many practices that are obstacles to positive change, and you as the leader can use reflective follow-up conversations to problem solve with your instructional team in order to eliminate those roadblocks and make the most of the opportunity to successfully deliver learning in your school. Don't focus exclusively on the classroom when there are additional changes needed at the building or organizational level.

DECIDING WHEN TO INTERVENE: THE MARGINAL TEACHER

One of the most critical and troublesome responsibilities of administrators is dealing with marginal teachers. However, the job is manageable if the walk-through process is used under the right conditions. First, you need to know that there is no constructive way to separate the walk-through observation process and its products from the overall evaluation process, and there is a fine line between a professional growth orientation and a summative evaluation orientation. However, there is a way for professional development and evaluation to be complementary. To be effective, it's important for you to know when to intervene and how to do it effectively.

A roadblock is created when reflective support and assistance is confused with summative evaluation for intervention with marginal teachers. In walk-through strategies, the aim is to see if the frequent visits trigger thoughts about reflective questions that would enhance a teacher's cognitive understanding of the decisions he or she makes and to provide professional enhancements in the teacher's practices. The teacher is in the driver's seat on changing behavior, so don't assume that if you mention something, it will automatically generate a favorable response. Your job is to get the teacher to think about his or her teaching practices and choices surrounding the practices you raise (see Chapter 3 for more on this topic).

With the expanded data obtained with the walk-through process, you will know more than you have ever known before about a teacher's decisions because you are visiting classrooms frequently. Your data on teacher performance will be deeper and more accurate, and your ability to assure that all classrooms are staffed with competent and functionally effective teachers will be enhanced.

A better and broader understanding of teachers' choices, practices, and work may occasionally lead you to the point of making difficult decisions about some teacher behaviors. When to step out of reflective questioning and into more directive forms of assistance is a tough judgment call, but consider the following factors before moving to an intervention mode with a teacher:

- First, is the teacher truly marginal? Consider these questions to find out:

  1. Are you spending a lot of time in that teacher's classroom? If you are continuously in that room because of a need to intervene in problems, it might mean serious trouble.

  2. Are you frequently motivated to give feedback? Are most of your comments designed for refinement rather than reinforcement? If most visits prompt you to offer some necessary feedback and/or highlight some skill that needs improvement or refinement, it may mean that further corrective action is required.

  3. Are your conversations with the teacher directive on your part rather than probing? If so, you may have a dependent relationship to resolve before you can move to reflection.

- What are the predispositions of the teacher? Is the teacher cooperative? Is the teacher open about problems in the classroom and welcoming toward your support and help? If not—or worse, if the teacher refuses to accept responsibility for inadequate performance—then you may have to move to interventionist strategies and professional-growth planning with that teacher.

In the intervention mode, the rules for walk-throughs change. Walk-through visits will need to be very frequent, if not continuous, and feedback will need to be characterized as frank in tone and direct in counsel. Probing questions are not advisable, and the specifically diagnosed skill deficiencies observed in the teacher should become the focus of your conversation. Teach to the teacher's weaknesses and inadequate skills. In effect, you become the teacher's teacher. You can do nothing more important than this in your job as instructional leader.

Of course, it goes without saying that all observations, discussions, coaching sessions, and relevant anecdotes for marginal employees may need to be documented to support any future action. You are doing no one any favors by beating around the bush or failing to take responsible administrative action to note problems and deficiencies observed (including time, date, and circumstances), guidance provided, suggestions given, and results achieved. Many marginal teachers, except perhaps those few who disdain feedback or repudiate any responsibility for observed problems, can be helped and rescued, given the right supervision, direction, and support.

EXAMPLES OF SUCCESSFUL IMPLEMENTATION: MAKING THE WALK-THROUGH PROCESS WORK

In the past several years, thousands of people have been trained in the walk-through and reflective inquiry approach. Many of them have been extremely successful in going back to their school systems and making the process a positive force in improving school achievement. Successful changes in school culture have built on the Downey process, which calls for facilitating teachers who are performing well in their practice to continuously consider their practices. In a sense, it becomes a culture where the leader is "giving strength to the strong," because this type of leader gives the kind of nonjudgmental food for thought that justifies the trust of the teachers (followers) (Greenleaf, 1996).

Salinas Union High School District, California

In Salinas, California, Roger Anton, Associate Superintendent of the Salinas Union High School District, provided training and several practicums for the district's principals and assistant principals. Following the training and field-experience application, he visited school sites for at least one-half day during each quarter for the purpose of coaching the principal and assistant principals in the process. This follow-up day began with a brief review of the status of walk-throughs in the visited building.

In Salinas Union High School, all site administrators were encouraged to spend at least 40 percent of instructional time in classrooms monitoring the implementation of the district curriculum and noting instructional practices. The principals were supposed to act as "coaches" for the teachers, and it was essential that they used the process in strict accordance with the Downey five-step observation structure.

After brief dialogue and teaching, the associate superintendent and principal visited classrooms for an hour, pausing between rooms to debrief about what was observed and to practice the five-step observation structure as well as the reflective question. This was perceived as an opportune time to hone the skills of principals in the following areas of professional service:

- Identification of the objective being taught (content, context, and cognitive type)
- Implementation of instructional practices that promote increased student achievement
- Selection of a possible teaching practice for follow-up conversation with a teacher (if a follow-up conversation was to occur)

After an hour with the principal, each of the assistant principals joined the visiting team (one at a time) for an hour each with the associate superintendent and the principal. The team of three continued this pattern of visiting classrooms and debriefing between visits.

Usually, the half day of practice involved visits by the team of site administrators to 35 or more classrooms. This provided the associate superintendent with an opportunity to coach the administrative staff during actual visitations, and through this process, patterns within the district's administrative staff, whether by site or district, became apparent. From these coaching opportunities, the associate superintendent was able to retrain personnel on specific skills, design additional training based on the observed needs, and monitor the effectiveness of the process.

Norman Public Schools, Norman, Oklahoma

Jean Cate and Linda Atkinson were early participants in the walk-through training program for potential trainers and mentors. They were able to use the process effectively and implement it early in the Norman Schools. Cate observed that the walk-through strategy gave principals and curriculum supervisors a quick structure with which to monitor the teaching of the district curriculum for alignment of the written and taught curriculum. The strategy also included the consideration of a reflective conversation about teaching content and practices, a powerful job-embedded staff development tool.

After training by the school system, principals began walking through classrooms in pairs, observing curriculum and instruction. It was also pointed out that in just one year, principals demonstrated the capability of learning 60 percent of the district curriculum through this process, which Cate feels is justification enough for administrative training in the processes (Cate, 2002). Principals who can identify the connection between the written/tested curriculum and what teachers are teaching are better able to strengthen deep curriculum alignment in their schools.

Durham and Simcoe County School Boards, Ontario, Canada

In the Durham and Simcoe County School Boards, near Toronto in Ontario, Canada, the walk-through process has been under way for a few years. Beverly Freedman, Durham Superintendent, and Clay LaFleur, Simcoe County Superintendent, reported that the process has been working very well in Canadian classrooms, not only in both school boards (i.e., districts) but in other communities as well (Freedman & LaFleur, 2002).

In Durham and Simcoe County School Boards, elementary and secondary principals received an initial training workshop on the school walk-through and were involved in a variety of follow-up activities related to the walk-through approach. Twenty principals were studied one year after they initiated the program in their schools. The results are reported below.

Coincidentally, the Ontario Education Act and its regulations (1998) mandated administrators to supervise instruction and to advise and assist teachers, so the walk-through process was timely and appropriate.

The walk-through process assisted principals in developing instructional leadership skills in their schools. Training was completed in two days and included time spent in actual classrooms along with discussion and reflection among the participants. Principals were trained to spend two- to four-minute intervals observing and listening in teachers' classrooms. In order to tighten the emphasis on curriculum instruction, the training focused on determining alignment between the written and taught curriculum, the type of instructional strategies, modes of classroom assessment, and levels of student engagement. Frequent and multiple visits to classrooms were encouraged. In particular, administrators spent time learning and practicing the art of reflective questioning using the data gathered from their visits to classrooms over time (Freedman & LaFleur, 2002). Freedman and LaFleur observed that the walk-through "heightened principals' visibility in classrooms and allowed principals to be recognized as instructional leaders."

Follow-up activities were provided for principals as well. Focused discussions were held with staff as well as with other principals about walk-through experiences. After a field trial lasting nearly a year, principals were interviewed to elicit their perceptions of the process and its level of success. Twenty principals from two districts reported in their interviews the following changes in patterns and themes within their schools (Freedman & LaFleur, 2002):

- Visibility of principals around the school increased.
- Curriculum was given stronger focus.

- The principal's role was reconsidered and modified.
- The school culture became more positive.
- Principals' comfort level with nonjudgmental reflective questioning improved over time.
- Time to conduct the walk-throughs remained an obstacle.

In addition, Freedman and LaFleur reported that the walk-throughs helped principals become more knowledgeable about the mandated curriculum expectations and enabled them to see firsthand the complexities of implementing the curriculum.

The experience in Ontario indicated that a deep, meaningful change had occurred in the school culture. When principals began actively visiting classrooms, the teachers' perceptions of the principal were enhanced in terms of the instructional leadership role. The strengthening of working relationships also resulted, and teachers became engaged in more relevant and specific discussions with principals.

Napa Valley Schools, Napa Valley, California

Olive McArdle-Kulas, Assistant Superintendent in the Napa Valley School District in California, reported that implementation of the walk-through process has dramatically changed the way the system operates. In order to build an emphasis on the walk-through process, she held her monthly curriculum meetings with principals at a given school site. For the first half hour of the meeting, principals visited classrooms using the walk-through protocol, and the next half hour was devoted to debriefing the lessons observed and planning different types of follow-up conversations.

Partners shared with the whole group, and together the group refined the recommended follow-up for the teacher(s). This variety of live experiences in analyzing lessons and designing effective follow-up conversations provided an unusually potent and continuous honing of principals' skills. Principals reported that this monthly support strengthened their confidence in using the reflective dialogue model with teachers and enabled them to develop better and more useful skills of observation, analysis, and follow-up conversation.

Shawnee Mission School District, Shawnee Mission, Kansas

In school year 2002–2003, the Shawnee Mission School District began the third year of an ongoing administrative professional development program called "Focus on Achievement." All 77 building administrators plus other administrative staff participated on a monthly basis. In the prior two years, all administrators had received formal walk-through coaching training. Each year, the implementation of walk-through techniques was required as one of the principals' annual performance objectives. "Focus on Achievement" sessions addressed walk-through implementation, and practice sessions were organized on a regular basis. Building administrators with a high level of skills served as group leaders during the practice sessions to bolster peer-to-peer coaching.

Gene Johnson, Associate Superintendent, reports that the response to this effort has been very positive, especially with the administrators who have implemented reflective questioning. Principals report that they are building a level of trust with their staffs and are finding teachers willing and asking to participate. A spirit of professionalism now permeates the schools and the relationship between staff and principal.

Bill Harrington, Principal of Shawnee Mission Northwest High School (2002 Blue Ribbon School), reported that administrators have discovered the value of practicing as an administrative team. He reported that the immediate debriefing following three- to four-minute visits in classrooms has proven to be extremely positive. The administrative staff's commitment to practice has led them to be quite comfortable with the process. Reflective questioning has proven invaluable.

It was reported that teachers were much more willing to listen to and accept what was being asked by principals. Teacher responses were very well thought out and focused on instructional issues. The discussion among the faculty resulted in teachers becoming much more aware of the walk-through process and made the administrative time in the classroom anticipated and worthwhile.

Columbia-Brazoria Independent School District, Texas

Cole Pugh, Superintendent of the Columbia-Brazoria Independent School District in Texas, provided principals with walk-through training in 2000–2001. The activity produced a highly beneficial educational and political effect. Walk-through supervision, along with some deep curriculum alignment activities, resulted in the school district improving from "Acceptable" to "Exemplary" in the Texas accountability system.

After the initial training was provided to principals, follow-up sessions were also scheduled. Central office personnel conducted walk-throughs with the principals, and they shared their findings and feedback recommendations afterward with one another. Principals were also asked to pair up with principals from other campuses and conduct classroom-monitoring activities with one another on their own. Principals were asked to share these walk-through experiences and some of their reflective questions during formative and summative appraisals. Pugh, who has moved on to the San Angelo Independent School District, reported that the process improved the relationship between principals and teachers and that the revitalized focus on curriculum had a very strong beneficial effect on student achievement.

San Leandro Unified School District, California

Pat Dickson, Associate Superintendent in the San Leandro Unified School District, an urban district in Northern California, reports that the walk-through process has been implemented in three important ways in this district.

The first approach involved training all site administrators, administrators at the district level who supervised them, and other support personnel from the areas of curriculum and instruction. Initial training was followed by frequent guided practice and coaching from the district administration.

From the beginning, some of the walk-through process and implementation strategies were incorporated into the principals' meetings, and once every other month all principals and district staff met at a site and practiced walk-throughs in pairs or small groups. A big challenge was to keep the principals focused on the objective being taught and on its relationship to the district-adopted standards.

The second component centered on a "debriefing" process used when principals visit and observe classrooms together. During the debriefing that follows walk-throughs, principals dug into the portable "black box" (a collection containing the scope and sequence for each of the curricular areas) and asked each other the following questions:

- Where does this fit in the adopted curriculum?
- How do the learnings spiral or connect across the system?
- Are we providing practice in multiple contexts aligned to the ways in which students will be assessed?

Principals also practiced the preparation and delivery of reflective questions related to what they've observed and followed this with a discussion of the challenges and successes they've experienced in having follow-up conversations with teachers at individual sites.

The cultural impact upon the organization was based on one powerful component—the common experience shared by principals and district administrators. Moreover, principals and other administrators became more familiar with the nature of the taught curriculum and instructional practices. A new focus emerged in the form of a recurring question: "How are we building a coherent educational system that serves the needs of *all* students?"

Dickson and the superintendent, Tom Himmelberg, also found the process useful in the supervision of principals. Consequently, they now schedule joint periodic walk-throughs throughout the year with each principal. As the team visits classrooms, reflective questions are discussed and principals are asked about the issues they are dealing with in becoming effective instructional leaders.

The final component of the San Leandro Schools process was focused on system monitoring of the implementation and delivery of the authorized curriculum. Dickson and three administrators in the Educational Services Division regularly scheduled walk-throughs at schools. Through these visits to classrooms at each site (assuring coverage at each grade level), the team monitored the implementation of the curriculum and observed firsthand the challenges teachers face as they implement the standards, use the district-developed curriculum guides and assessments, and practice the strategies they have learned in professional development sessions. The focus of this team was centered on the following questions:

- What are the implications of what we are seeing for our work in classrooms?
- How can we provide better support to teachers?
- Where are the models within our district that we can use to provide examples for teachers throughout the district?

In the San Leandro Schools, this three-pronged approach has proven to be a powerful tool in focusing attention throughout the entire system on what really needs to happen in the classroom. A substantial cultural shift has emerged in the system, characterized by a shared sense of responsibility among the whole administrative team for the improvement of instruction at all levels and for *all* students. Most important, it honors the incredibly difficult work that teachers do and underscores the key role that administrators must play in providing meaningful follow-up conversation and support to help teachers become better over time at delivering learning.

San Benito County, California, County Office of Education

Another example of effective implementation is found in how a county Office of Education assisted school district leadership in carrying out the walk-through approach in districts. Susan Villa, Assistant Superintendent of the San Benito County Office of Education, worked with the administrators of the Hollister Elementary School District in California on a monthly basis to review the walk-through process and the use of reflective questions. Each month, Dr. Villa conducted a review session where everyone shared their experiences, talked about curriculum alignment with the standards, and practiced reflective questions. It was noteworthy that the walk-through process quickly became routine for the administrators.

She reported that, "It was very exciting to have one of the middle school principals practically jump out of her seat to announce that all the classrooms she had observed that week had curriculum that was aligned with the standards."

For most of the administrators, however, the reflective question remained elusive. It was realized early on that administrators needed more guided practice, so the facilitator used some of the principals' observations to guide them in their practice of reflective questioning. It was very helpful to have the scenarios come from actual observations. By the end of the year, the majority of the administrators were able to do a reflective question with minimal coaching.

CULTIVATING THE CULTURE: A FINAL WORD

Using the five-step walk-through observation structure with reflective questioning in your school involves a good deal more than simply implementing a new administrative strategy—it is an extraordinary commitment to change. More important, the change is transformational—it modifies and transforms the system's culture. Implementation of the walk-through process produces several unifying elements that characterize the transformed system, including the following expectations and results:

- The greater visibility of principals around their schools will have a salutary and beneficial impact on learning and achievement (Frase, 2001).
- School leaders will provide a new voice—a voice of knowledge and experience in improving curriculum delivery, learning, and achievement (Freedman & LaFleur, 2002).
- Principals begin to wear a new hat—that of instructional leader. For many, this will be foreign at first, but teachers will eventually recognize how the role of the principal has changed. Moreover, teachers will begin to welcome the change in their leader's behavior (Freedman & LaFleur, 2002).

- Achievement gaps and shortcomings in high-stakes testing environments will be minimized over time, given a culture where walk-through observations and curriculum monitoring are the custom (English & Steffy, 2001).

There is much benefit to be obtained from a cultural shift that embodies the walk-through with reflective inquiry process—schools, educational organizations, administrators, and principals all have much to gain. The persistent problems confronting education in terms of achievement deficits and gaps remain difficult challenges for educational leaders, but the likelihood of overcoming these problems is improved with a culture that includes the power of the walk-through. The walk-through process is a step—a very big step—in the right direction for the improvement of teaching and learning. Every step toward the transformation of school culture by utilizing the Downey Walk-Through process brings hope and efficacy to the future of education.

Using the Walk-Through Process to Promote a Collaborative, Reflective Culture

When the Downey Walk-Through process is fully implemented in a school, we believe the culture of the school will change and become one that could be described as collaborative and reflective. Further, we feel the communication practices between teachers and administrators used in the model go beyond what is commonly considered good supervisory practice and become more inquiry based. This inquiry-based collaboration is the outcome of implementing the two main parts of the walk-through process: frequent, short classroom visits, and conversations with teachers about how and why teachers make the decisions they do when planning, implementing, and evaluating their teaching.

The basic assumptions undergirding the process include the following:

- Teachers seek ways to grow and develop over time.
- Teachers benefit from engaging in reflective dialogue.
- Principals play a key role in facilitating teacher growth and reflection.
- The culture of a school is greatly influenced by teacher and principal behavior.

Take a few minutes to reflect on these assumptions and record your thoughts below.

REFLECTION

Do You Agree or Disagree With These Assumptions?

(Write your comments here.)

_____

_____

_____

_____

While there has always been an intent for supervision to lead to the creation of a collaborative, inquiry-based culture, this has not generally happened.

EARLY HISTORY

The professionalization of supervision has been plagued by the same problems facing the evolution of other professions. "The concept of professionalism implies readiness to replace any theoretical idea or practice, no matter how time-honored, with one found to be more valid. Yet this principle is often violated, and inherited outlooks and practices continue to operate. This is one of supervision's greatest problems" (Tanner & Tanner, 1987, p. 4). Over the years, many teachers and administrators have become cynical about supervision, and we believe it may be time to replace the word. In its early beginnings, between 1620 and 1850, supervision was inspectional in nature. Those inspecting could be clergy, selectmen, or members of citizens committees. They inspected schools to be sure that rules were followed and that children were being provided with an adequate education. They looked for deficiencies. A typical inspection had the supervisor riding up to the one-room schoolhouse and asking a student to read a section of the Bible. While another purpose of these early visitations was to ensure the improvement of teaching, there was mixed practice among the early inspectors about how this was to be achieved.

As reported by Tanner and Tanner, (1987 pp. 8–27), the legacy of supervision from the early years included the following:

1. Public responsibility for schooling was unprecedented in the world at that time.

2. Colonists had to work out the details of how it would work.

3. America had compulsory education.

4. Supervision was initially concerned with seeing to it that parents sent their children to school.

5. Providing educational opportunities for all children was a departure from the system used in England.

6. Improvement of instruction was a primary goal for supervision.

7. States achieved control over supervision.

8. The graded school, the superintendency, and education organizations evolved.

9. By the 1800s, school supervision was dubbed "mechanical and suitable only for producing automatons, not for developing self-directing citizens of the republic" (p. 12).

10. Local school autonomy grew.

11. The first state board was established in Massachusetts in 1826.

12. The state fiduciary control demanded state supervision. "It is important to understand clearly that one reason why educational reformers sought state supervision was the poor quality of supervision at the local level" (p. 16).

13. Teacher licensure requirements did not guarantee teacher competence.

The job description of a teacher was similar to the one presented below, which was adopted by the Harrison, South Dakota, Board of Education in 1872 (Oliva & Pawlas, 1997, p. 7).

Instruction to the Teacher

- *Teachers will fill lamps, clean chimneys, and trim wicks each day.*
- *Each teacher will bring a scuttle of coal and a bucket of water for day's use.*
- *Make your pens carefully. You may whittle nibs for the individual tastes of children.*

- *Men teachers may take one evening each week for courting purposes or two evenings a week if they go to church regularly.*
- *After ten hours in school, the teacher should spend the remaining time reading the Bible and other good books.*
- *Women teachers who marry or engage in other unseemly conduct will be dismissed.*
- *Every teacher should lay aside from every pay a goodly sum of his earnings for his declining years so that he will not become a burden on society.*
- *Any teacher who smokes, uses liquor in any form, frequents pool or public halls, or gets shaved in a barbershop will give good reason to suspect his worth, intentions, integrity and honesty.*
- *The teacher who performs his labors faithfully without fault for five years will be given an increase of 25 cents a week in his pay [providing the Board of Education approved].*

(Reprinted by permission of the Board of Education, Harrison, South Dakota, Anglin, Goldman, & Anglin, 1982.)

According to Tanner and Tanner, not only did the licensure procedure fail to protect the public against incompetent teachers, the work teachers performed was often terribly demeaning, as reflected in the job description above. By 1839, the first normal school was established in the United States, and by 1900 all states had some form of teacher preparation. As the complexity of schools expanded, so, too, did the role of professional supervision. As the role moved from lay committees to the superintendent, there was a greater focus on school visitations by the superintendent and on general meetings with teachers. At these meetings, teachers commonly heard from outside speakers, became aware of professional literature, and discussed new classroom practices.

Between 1850 and 1910, new school principal positions were added. These positions were seen as an opportunity for improvement of instruction. The inspectional role was still in place, but there was an expanded interest in helping teachers improve. During much of the past century, we have seen an expansion of central-office positions to include general and special central-office supervisors. During the 1910 to 1930 period there was an interest in making schools more efficient. After that we saw the emergence of human relations orientations and democratic forms of supervision. By 1975, supervision encompassed ideas such as scientific management, clinical supervision, collaboration, peer coaching, group dynamics, mentoring, and the teacher as artist. During this era, supervisors began to realize that their role had become dependent upon their relationship with teachers (Oliva & Pawlas, 1997). They recognized their role as that of responding to the needs of the teachers they served. Supervisor positions were established to help teachers improve instruction in particular areas. These were commonly staff positions. Typically, a district would employ one supervisor to work with hundreds of teachers. The evaluation of teachers remained the domain of the building principal, and there was a conscious effort to separate the two functions.

What we are seeing today is an amalgamation of practices and attitudes. True, we can find holdovers of the inspection mentality, and we still encounter the boss-employee mind-set, but we are experiencing more cases of cooperation and collaboration between supervisors and teachers than in the past. We find a definite acceptance of the idea that instructional supervisors are employed to help teachers build on their strengths, improve, and remain in the profession, rather than to probe teachers' deficiencies and seek their dismissal.

Spend a few minutes reflecting about your view of how supervision has changed over the past 10 to 20 years. Write your comments in the space provided.

REFLECTION

How Do You Think Supervision
Has Changed Over the Past 10 to 20 Years?

_____

_____

_____

_____

Today supervision may take many forms, and it is difficult to find an agreed-upon definition of exactly what it is. For many teachers, it is viewed more negatively than positively. That is why we recommend abolishing the term.

In the past, teacher evaluation was often seen as a separate function, apart from the daily functioning of the school. It was grounded in contract language and became the mechanism for producing summative evaluations that were formally written, signed by the teacher and principal, and placed in confidential personnel files. A newly hired teacher could expect to undergo three to five of these observations per year for the first two or three years of employment. After that, the number and frequency of these observations was typically reduced to one every two to three years.

Over the years, our team has had an opportunity to conduct studies of many school systems in this country. As part of this process, we request a random sample of teacher evaluations that have had all forms of personal identification removed. Overwhelmingly, these evaluations are positive and the teachers are rated as satisfactory or above. For instance, if the evaluation was a checklist and the teachers were rated on a scale of 1 to 5 with 5 being the highest, most teachers receive a rating of 4 or 5. If a narrative is included, the statements are usually general in nature and complimentary (Frase & Streshly, 1994).

We have found overwhelmingly positive teacher evaluations in schools where large numbers of students are failing, where many students cannot read at grade level and do not meet state standards, and where half of the students entering 9th grade do not graduate. Something is wrong with this picture. Our old practices of supervision and evaluation of teachers have failed to produce schools where the majority of students can read at grade level, where a large percentage of students meet state standards, and where most students entering 9th grade eventually graduate from high school. There has been a disconnect between supervisory assessments and what students know and are able to accomplish.

Fortunately, there is a movement under way that goes beyond these ineffective practices toward a model that combines instructional supervision, ongoing professional development, coaching and mentoring, and adult learning. We have termed this new approach *collaborative, reflective dialogue.* It is exemplified in the walk-through with reflective dialogue model. As explained in earlier chapters of this book, the success of this model is dependent upon the frequent presence of the building principal in classrooms. During these visits, principals are collecting data that focus on whether the teacher is implementing the district curriculum and using effective, research-based instructional practices. Clearly, the most powerful part of the model is in the reflective, collaborative dialogue that follows the visit.

In the next section of this chapter, we will trace the development of practices that have contributed to the linkage between the walk-through process and its potential for leading to the creation of a collaborative, reflective culture.

DEVELOPMENTAL SUPERVISION AND MENTORING

First, the role of supporting the classroom teacher has expanded beyond the building principal. Many positions have been created to support the classroom teacher; these include content area coordinators, principals and assistant principals, teacher specialists, instructional lead teachers, mentors, and others who have the responsibility of ensuring that all children are achieving at high levels.

Take a moment to reflect upon all of the positions in your district that are designed to provide support for the classroom teacher.

REFLECTION

List all of the support positions that
exist in your district and describe the primary
functions carried out by each of these positions.

_____

_____

_____

_____

Unfortunately, the job responsibilities of these support positions are not well defined, and there is little communication across roles about how to coordinate activities among these positions or programs. For example, these support positions could include reading specialists, resource teachers, instructional lead teachers, tutors, and paraprofessionals. With the enactment of No Child Left Behind legislation, there has been some effort on the part of schools and districts to coordinate programs across funding sources. For most districts, this effort is still at the formative stage. Many districts are still trying to figure out how to meet the requirements of No Child Left Behind, let alone how to coordinate services.

Nevertheless, effective supervisory practices have long been linked to successful schools (Glickman, Gordon, & Ross-Gordon, 1995). The walk-through process focuses on the role of the principal but expands, over time, to include all of these support positions. The bottom line is that teachers need direct, differentiated, sustained assistance (Reiman & Thies-Sprinthall, 1998). This idea is not a new one. It can be traced to the work of John Dewey, who emphasized that teacher learning and growth do not magically and spontaneously unfold. Rather, teachers depend on appropriate inter-action between themselves and the principal and between themselves and other professionals. We would underscore that teacher learning and growth are dependent upon the interaction between teacher and principal.

For many years, supervisory practice has been linked to the work of Morris Cogan, who created the clinical supervisory model in 1950. Over the years, we have often focused on the steps in the process and somehow forgotten the original intent of the Cogan model. Cogan was always concerned with the viewpoint of the teacher and what the teacher was thinking when he or she made decisions.

Clinical supervision is conceptualized as much as possible from the teacher's viewpoint. That is, it is primarily shaped to be congruent with the teacher's universe, with his or her internal landscape, rather than with that of the supervisor (Cogan, 1973).

This imperative is a cornerstone of the Downey Walk-Through process: The walk-through process is centered on the teacher, not the principal. It is a growth experience and another form of teaching that requires thought-ful dialogue. We view this model as one exemplifying developmental supervision with origins traced to people such as Dewey and Cogan and disciplines such as psychology, philosophy, and sociology, as well as education.

Reiman and Thies-Sprinthall (1998) have defined differential super-vision as follows:

> An in-class and in-school process for refining and expanding instruc-tional repertoire that accounts for and differentiates between support and challenge according to the teachers' individual learning and developmental needs. Such a process promotes both individual and school-wide change, learning, and growth. (p. 6)

It is our position that it is this differential supervision that helps create the collaborative, reflective culture. This process is formative in nature; that is, it extends over a period of time and requires a trustful relationship between the teacher and the principal. Trustful relationships with staff are a precursor to differentiated supervision. These relationships are built over time, they are reciprocal, and they operate with a large degree of confidentiality. Most of us have a professional friend or two with whom we can engage in honest dialogue. These relationships are highly valuable. We turn to these trusted colleagues to share problems, brainstorm solutions, and seek advice. The differentiated supervisory role between a principal and a teacher has many of the same characteristics. The principal has the additional role of summative evaluation. This is of a formal nature, usually mandated by state law and regulations and used to determine continued employability status. There was a time when it was felt that a principal could not perform both a formative and a summative role. Now it is believed that the role of the principal in formative evaluation complements and enhances the summative role. The formative role enables the principal to have a broader view of the ongoing instructional activity in a teacher's classroom. This context and the dialogue about instruction the principal has experienced with a teacher enable the principal to conduct a more holistic, comprehensive, summative evaluation. We also know that when a principal is actively involved in formative, differentiated supervision, teachers are more willing to accept summative accounts as true representations of their abilities.

The principal engaged in differentiated supervision is, in many ways, acting as a mentor. This is a two-way relationship grounded in a true partnership philosophy. It can be described as a power-free facilitation of learning. As Chip Bell (1998) would say,

> It is about teaching through consultation and affection rather than constriction and assessment. (p. xi)

> Effective mentors are like friends in that their goal is to create a safe context for growth. (p. 7)

> The best mentors recognize that they are, first and foremost, facilitators and catalysts in a process of discovery and insight, and mentors practice their skills with a combination of never-ending compassion, crystal-clear communication, and a sincere joy in the role of being a helper along a journey toward mastery. (p. 8)

This is a role most building principals have never been trained to assume. Some come to it naturally. Others must be trained to assume this role. However they achieve it, it is an essential role for creating a collaborative, reflective culture.

What practices does your current supervisor use that you feel support your professional growth and what practices inhibit your growth? List them below.

```
                              REFLECTION

Supervisory Practices That          Supervisory Practices That
Support Your Professional           Interfere With Your
Professional
Growth                              Growth

_____

_____

_____

```

THE TEACHER AS AN ADULT LEARNER

For many years, the idea of adult learning was ignored. Adulthood was thought to be a stable phase of life, and whatever characteristics adults possessed could be traced to childhood experiences. As noted by Heist and Yonge in 1968, "The ability for reflective thought, the use of abstractions, and problem solving, is fixed by the age of 17" (p. 2). These beliefs changed with the work of Baltes and Schaie (1976), who showed that inductive reasoning, spatial ability, and verbal ability grew well into adulthood. Snarey (1985) found that adults showed growth in both ego or self-development and moral judgment. The work of these researchers and many others laid the foundation for viewing the cognitive development of adults in a different manner.

Reiman and Thies-Sprinthall (1998) have outlined the following series of key propositions that guide cognitive developmental theory (p. 41):

1. All persons process experience through cognitive structures.

2. Cognitive structures are organized in a hierarchical sequence of stages or plateaus from the less complex to the more complex.

3. Each shift in stage represents a major transformation in how the person makes meaning from his or her experience.

4. Development is not automatic.

5. Behaviors can be determined and predicted by a person's particular stage of development.

When these propositions are applied to the adult-to-adult reflective dialogue in the Downey model, it is clear that this interchange is constructivist in nature. Teachers make meaning based on their lived experiences. Meaning changes as they reflect about experience. The process takes place over time with peaks and plateaus of growth. It is gradual and can be accelerated and supported through dialogue that brings to consciousness deeply held beliefs that often reside at the subconscious level. During the career of a teacher, the thought processes about knowing become more complex. The newly certified teacher may need help in learning how to build the mental scaffolding necessary for continued adult cognitive growth. The building principal plays a pivotal role in promoting this.

While a number of theorists have studied the area of cognitive development, we will mention three here: Hunt (1971), Loevinger (1976), and Kohlberg (1969). Hunt was influential for his work on how people solved problems in situations involving human interaction. He concluded that teachers who operated at higher conceptual levels were more effective. "They were more adaptive in teaching style, more flexible, and more tolerant of ambiguity" (Reiman & Thies-Sprinthall, 1998, p. 44). Hunt termed these more complex behaviors as responsiveness, reciprocality, and reflexivity. The following is the three-stage conceptual model Hunt envisioned (pp. 44–45):

Stage A: Concrete Conceptual Level

Thinking tends to be concrete. Rules are considered fixed and unalterable. There is a preference for the single "tried-and-true" approach to teaching. Pleasing others is desirable. There is a strong preference for highly structured learning activities.

Stage B: Concrete/Abstract Conceptual Level

There is a greater awareness of alternative strategies for solving problems as well as a growing awareness of the importance of feelings. Teachers are more open to new ideas and can tolerate some ambiguity.

Stage C: Abstract Conceptual Level

Teachers weigh and balance alternatives, take risks, value collaboration, and exhibit evidence of synthesis and integration in complex intellectual and interpersonal functions. There is a full self-acceptance of the teacher's behavior. Teachers can "read and flex" with students and employ a large repertoire of teaching strategies.

Hunt was a strong proponent of the need to differentiate learning strategies for teachers.

Loevinger developed a series of stages of ego development. Ego was thought to be the gatekeeper for directing a person's actions. At higher stages of ego development, the teacher is more aware of the complexity of a situation, can deal with greater degrees of ambiguity, and can choose from an expanded array of possible choices. A few of the stages in Loevinger's model include the labels "symbiotic-impulsive," where a teacher is dependent and can experience conceptual confusion; "conscientious-conformist," where a teacher is able to balance the needs of self and the needs of the group (teachers at this stage can balance and differentiate among competing goals and norms); and "autonomous," where a teacher is able to tolerate conflict between the self and the social context. A teacher at this level displays a high degree of autonomy and self-awareness.

Kohlberg's model explains how a person thinks about social justice. The model has three levels: the "pre-conventional level," based on the notion of trading or exchanging favors; the "conventional level," where what the majority of people want or what the law dictates determines behavior; and the "post-conventional level," where decisions are based on principles (p. 47).

All of these theories of cognitive growth inform our supervisory practices. From them we know that not all teachers are at the same level of cognitive growth, and because of this they need differentiated approaches to learning. At the higher levels of cognitive growth, teachers appear to be able to tolerate higher degrees of ambiguity, are more autonomous, and are better at reasoning, communicating ideas, and processing information.

So how does all of this relate to the principal's role in assisting teacher growth and development? Left alone, teachers have difficulty promoting their own growth. Without assistance, a few teachers can promote their own growth and development, but the vast majority of them do not have these skills. Consequently, the majority of teachers working in classrooms today do not have the skills necessary to question their behavior, reflect about practice, seek out new knowledge, and change their practice so that more children are learning at high levels. Add to this the classroom arena where demographics are changing at a remarkable speed. Within the next few years, classrooms will be filled with a majority of minority children. The current cadre of teachers is ill prepared to deal with this scenario, and without the assistance of a strong instructional leader, they will remain frustrated and ill equipped to meet the needs of this new generation of students. Changing practice is essential to meeting the needs of these students. The problem is not that these students cannot learn; the problem is that old methods and procedures will not do the job. Part of the answer to this problem resides in the mind and abilities of the building principal. Can this individual engage teachers in thoughtful dialogue leading to growth? We believe this can happen, and we believe the Downey model of walk-throughs is a key enabler.

PROMOTING DEVELOPMENT

Humans are naturally curious. Teachers are naturally curious, especially when it comes to being more effective in the classroom. Dewey was noted for realizing that the thinking teachers go through in planning, delivering, and evaluating current lessons is inextricably linked to their planning, implementation, and evaluation of future lessons. Dewey is famous for his belief in learning by doing. "His notions of interaction, continuity, experience and reflection, and growth through phases have guided much educational inquiry during the twentieth century" (Tanner & Tanner, 1987, p. 68). The key here is how to engage the teacher in reflective dialogue about past practice to inform future practice. That is the essence of the Downey model. It provides a mechanism to do just that. This model utilizes what Furth (1981) referred to as "relaxed reflection" as a key element to the disequilibrium felt in a growth experience. Reiman and Thies-Sprinthall (1998) summarized Furth's concept of the phases of developmental learning as follows:

1. Awareness of a moderate discrepancy arises in understanding the meaning of an event or idea.

2. A feeling of curiosity or uneasiness arises.

3. More new information accumulates that doesn't fit with prior understanding.

4. During periods of relaxed reflection, one tries to fit the new information into the prior perspective, talking to oneself.

5. A new balance is reached. The new information moves from accommodation to assimilation.

6. After sufficient time, the new information becomes "old" information and can be adapted to other situations.

7. A new moderate discrepancy or "perturbation" arises and the process of equilibration continues (p. 77).

Vygotsky (1962) is noted for stressing the importance of dialogue and discussion as a primary component of growth. He believed that through dialogue with others, more growth can happen than with an individual thinking alone. He identified a zone of proximal growth.

The zone is an arena of thought and feeling that is slightly ahead of the current equilibrium. Sometimes this is referred to as a minor discrepancy, a slight mismatch, or an arena of manageable dissonance. Cognitive growth occurs in this zone and thus requires both support and challenge. Too much support or support without challenge essentially creates a condition of no growth. A person may wish to avoid the upset feelings caused by the perturbation, resist the change, and remain in place. (p. 77)

It is in this arena that the skills of the principal, engaging in reflective dialogue with a teacher, must work. These are learned skills and probably the most difficult to master, since the vast majority of training most building principals receive is with the traditional inspection supervisory model.

Adding more depth to our understanding of teachers, within recent years there has been a growing body of work done on teacher career development (Fessler & Christensen, 1992; Huberman, 1993; Steffy, 1989; Steffy & Wolfe, 1997). Fessler and Christensen's model identified three spheres of influence in a teacher's life: personal, organizational, and the career cycle sphere. Personal influences include family situations, crises, and positive experiences. Organizational influences deal with the social context and include such things as public trust and societal expectations. The career cycle sphere identifies and labels chronological benchmarks over years in the profession: preservice, enthusiastic and growing, stable but stagnant, and career wind-down. Huberman's work is consistent with Fessler and Christensen's in that they all recognize the importance of social context and the fact that there is a cross-play between social context and maturational level. Steffy and Wolfe have added the concept of reflection as a key component for continued growth over time. The Steffy and Wolfe model is described in depth in Chapter 10 of this book, with an explanation of how it can be the basis for differentiated supervision utilizing the walk-through process.

These models are significant to our discussion of adult cognitive development because they extend and deepen our understanding of the complexity of human growth. Human growth and professional growth do not take place in a vacuum. Rather, social context, career stage, and level of maturity are all at play in how teachers make meaning from their experiences. The principal can serve as the catalyst for new growth as teachers confront the learning environment and strive to improve it.

Table 7.1 shows the characteristics of the traditional learning environment versus the environment created by collaborative, reflective dialogue.

Table 7.1   Comparison of Traditional Learning Environment With the Collaborative Reflective Learning Environment

Traditional Learning Environment	Collaborative Reflective Learning Environment
• Teacher growth and development is primarily left up to the initiative of the individual teacher. • While yearly goals are required as part of the development of a professional improvement plan, these are often too general in nature. • Teachers must seek feedback about progress during the year. • Principals do provide comments at the end of the year, usually in writing and the process begins again.	• The principal and teacher work much more in unison to promote each other's growth. • There is ongoing, informal dialogue about areas for growth, a mutual sharing of information, and frequent visits to the classroom. • Little is written down in a formal sense, but the depth of conversation is thoughtful and focused on connecting practice to improved student learning.
• Classrooms remain generally as they have over the years. • Instruction is closely dictated by the textbook. • There is a propensity to use lots of worksheets, and the most common instruction is direct and addressed to the total class.	• There is ample evidence of differentiated instruction to meet the individual needs of students. • Materials are varied and keyed to a variety of learning styles and levels. • There is evidence of student self-assessment and peer assessment as well as frequent teacher feedback.
• Students are passive, doing what the teacher directs them to do with little thought as to why.	• Students are active in selecting learning goals, seeking resources, and taking ownership of the products they produce.
• Students hand in work and teachers grade it. • There is little connection between the next assignment and the work just completed. • Students generally do not have an opportunity to dialogue with the teacher about errors or receive more guided support.	• There is frequent and varied use of data to inform practice. • Students and teachers rely on data to earmark specific instructional goals and determine progress toward these goals. • Students are able to track their progress over time through the use of scoring rubrics, test scores, and reflective journals. • Feedback is seen as a critical component in the learning process.

(Continued)

Table 7.1 (Continued)

Traditional Learning Environment	Collaborative Reflective Learning Environment
• Students are often apathetic and approach the learning environment with a half-hearted commitment. • There are few questions from students about assignments, nor are they given opportunities to choose how an instructional goal will be achieved.	• Teachers and students feel in control of the learning environment. • Students know that they can seek help and resources will be provided. • Students and teachers learn to critically assess what they are doing and look for ways to improve. • Questions about strategies and techniques are welcomed and can lead to critical problem solving.
• School reform is given lip service but actions tend to be directed at the need for change in family structures, parental support, and school discipline.	• School reform is taken seriously. • Educators seek solutions that change the internal functioning of schools and classrooms. • Teachers accept students as they are and change practice to meet their needs.

In this chapter, we have briefly traced the development of the concept of supervision. From the very beginnings of education in this country, there has always been a desire for supervisory practice to lead to improved instruction. We believe a key to achieving this goal is through the creation of a collaborative, reflective culture. As supervisors work to change their style of interaction with teachers, and then as teachers reflect on the way they think about instruction, together they end up profoundly changing classroom practice. So we see how the walk-through process contributes to fruitful collaboration.

Determining Whether Walk-Throughs Are the Right Stuff

8

As we sat down to write this book, we discussed the many innovations that we, school administrators and other educators, have adopted. The list became voluminous, and we naturally asked if any of it truly made a difference for students or public school education in general. It is not news that educational innovations come and go. Naturally, we educators want very much to improve education for our students. Today, when all educators are under tremendous pressure to make dramatic test score improvements, many hurry to grab the new products and programs parading at educational conferences and in the literature. These products are selected based on their promises and slick packaging—not on demonstrated results. Faddism reigns, and America's educational freeways are strewn with wrecks of the perpetrators' bandwagons. This has been the case for decades. One of us reflected on the implementation in 1968 of open education and multiage grouping in her school. She and the teachers bought the ideas hook, line, and sinker, because they promised great benefits. None of the teachers or the principal asked for proof or empirical data that justified the claims, but all were enthralled with the idea and its promises (Goodlad & Anderson, 1963). Did it work? Who could know; no one asked the question let alone collected data. This scenario has likely taken place in every school district in America.

The Hunter model is another example of faddishness. On the surface it appeared to make great sense—it offered the magic elixir, a formula for instructional excellence. The mantra of this program was, "Plan this way, and teach this way, and kids will learn more and better." The model truly was beautiful. Those of us who had the opportunity to participate in Hunter's seminars were awed by her rationale for the model, and to see her teach was an exhilarating experience. She indeed was possibly the best teacher in the history of American education. Her trainers spoke eloquently of the model's virtues, and they were very good at their craft. We were told that it had a research base in psychology, theories of learning, and student achievement. When asked for a bibliography documenting the research base, however, the trainers repeatedly responded with advertisements for additional training. The claimed research base was ill founded, and the Hunter model did not do what it promised—it did not produce greater student achievement than other instructional methods (Slavin, 1989). Scenarios like this abound (Ellis & Fouts, 1993) and include the bandwagon concepts of restructuring, team teaching, block scheduling, site-based decision making, and a host of others.

As we write this chapter introduction, we are reminded of the similarities between the birth and death of educational innovations and what the late Stephen J. Gould (2002) termed "punctuated equilibrium"—how species originate, persist over time, and die through extinction or new circumstances. It was large asteroid impacts that got the best of dinosaurs. Punctuated equilibrium also describes educational innovations—they appear on the scene, live an abbreviated life, and perish or lose their identity in favor of the next fad. The Hunter model evolved and made a big splash, it dominated other instructional models because it was more powerful (had greater appeal), and it is now near death due to the appearance of other more appealing or "sexy" innovations—and due to the fact that it failed to produce greater learning (Slavin, 1989). To round out the comparison, Slavin was to the Hunter model as giant asteroids were to the dinosaurs.

Please take a minute to do a personal reflection on the ideas presented above. Here are a few questions that will aid you (There is space for your detailed answers below the list of questions.):

1. What are your thoughts about the general ideas regarding innovations and faddism, the punctuated equilibrium analogy, and so on?

2. What innovations have you been involved with?

3. What is the status of each innovation now?

4. What evidence is available about the effects of each?

5. Did these have a valid research base?

6. How do you feel about all of this?

INNOVATIONS

(Write your reflections here.)

1. _____

2. _____

3. _____

4. _____

5. _____

6. _____

BACKGROUND AND HISTORY OF MANAGEMENT BY WANDERING AROUND

Walk-throughs are a refinement of management by wandering around, and effective leaders have practiced Management by Wandering Around (MBWA) throughout the ages. They did not call it MBWA, but they did wander throughout their organizations because they knew that was where the real work took place. Today, as in the past, MBWA leaders are out listening for hints and clues about strengths, weaknesses, problems, and solutions to problems their people are experiencing. They know that MBWA is about caring enough about what's going on to talk to the people who know. They also know that a crucial component of great leadership is acting on behalf of the wants, goals, needs, and aspirations of the people in the organization. Our esteemed 16th president, Abe Lincoln, is a great example. Abraham Lincoln managed directly. No secondhand report for the Civil War president; Lincoln spent much of his time among the troops. They were number one to him; they were the people who were going to get the job done. He met with the generals and cabinet members in their homes, offices, and in the field, principally to provide direction and leadership (McKenna, 1993). U.S. Secretary of State Colin Powell expressed his beliefs about MBWA during the Gulf War: When asked about his leadership style, he summed it up by saying, "Go where your flock is."

An example from the distant past comes from Alexander the Great. When it was clear that his Macedonians were mutinying against his plans with the Persians, Alexander went directly to his men and spoke to them. He did not send a "power memo" or a messenger. As H. G. Wells (1961) describes it, "with some difficulty . . . he brought them to a penitent mood and induced them to take part in a common feast with the Persians" (p. 292).

MBWA leaders do not retreat to the hallowed walls of their offices to cast aspersions or point fingers of blame at the minions in the tradition of Marie Antoinette and King Louis XVI, who settled into their comfy castle, drank wine, and ate bread in isolation from the people. As a result, they were beheaded. Not a good result!

The first formal practice of MBWA we have found in the professional literature is Hewlett-Packard (known as H-P in the 1970s) (Trueman, 1991). At that time, H-P provided training in MBWA and required its managers to practice it; that was before the popularity ignited by the ideas of Peters and Waterman (1984). Following this, MBWA exploded in the literature and in practice.

MBWA was formally introduced as an educational management theory in 1990 (Frase & Hetzel, 1990). At that time, there were very few research studies on MBWA, but it seemed to be a great idea, and many educators followed. Even nonmanagers believe in MBWA. Elliot Eisner, one of America's most highly respected thinkers in pedagogy, and one who comes from a nonmanagement leadership background, is in sync with MBWA and classroom walk-throughs. Eisner (2002) said that in the kind of schools America needs, principals would spend about a third of their time in classrooms so that they would know firsthand what is going on. Is one third the precise amount, or is it 40 or 50 percent? We have seen any percentage between 30 and 50 work—the key is what the administrator does while wandering. There is strong evidence that teachers, too, like to see their principals in classrooms (Frase, in press).

Today, the research base is expansive and deep; it shows diverse and highly desirable outcomes associated with MBWA. In other words, when administrators practice MBWA, *good things happen.*

Before proceeding with the research section, let's take a minute to think about the administrators we know who practice MBWA. Who are they and how would you feel about them being in your classroom?

Who Practices MBWA and How I Feel About It.

(Write your thoughts here.)

_____

_____

_____

_____

WHY ARE BOTH A RESEARCH AND A THEORY BASE NEEDED BEFORE ADOPTING AN INNOVATION?

What about the effects of MBWA? The good news is that the dark clouds that surround the educational innovations discussed in the last section do not apply to MBWA as presented in this book. Personally, we have witnessed the devastating but fully justified work of those who debunk the touted merits of programs based on methodological flaws. We do not wish to be subjected to such embarrassment. We want nothing to do with carpetbagging, hucksterism, or charlatanism. In this chapter, you will see just how MBWA does have a strong research and theory base.

Before we discuss the research, a few words about guidelines for accepting and rejecting innovations would be helpful. Ellis and Fouts (1993) did a fine job of providing the profession with guidelines for selecting worthy innovations to implement in our schools. Their major message is if there's not a research and theory base, *don't get too excited about the new elixir.* Lawler (1971) cleverly stated the need for both theory and research: "Theory without data is fantasy, but data without theory is chaos" (p. 205). *You can't have one without the other.*

There is a great difference between an isolated piece of knowledge gained from one experience or a very limited set of experiences, and a worthy theory. When knowledge is built into a theory, we can use it to reliably make predictions over time. When the theory is proven correct (such as when tested in research), the theory grows stronger. When the theory fails, it must be rejected or revised to make it more reliable. Strong theory is built through systematic observations and revision. In folklore, the barnyard rooster Chanticleer formed a theory that aggrandized his status in life. He observed that the sun rose every morning after he crowed and flapped his wings, so he surmised that the sunrise was a result of his wing-flapping. However, one morning he overslept and did not crow, and the sun still rose. Ego deflated, he had to revise his theory. Had Chanticleer challenged his initial theory, he would have tested it to see if the sun rose every day regardless of whether he flapped his wings or not. This is a silly but meaningful story. Chanticleer had untested data, yet he used it as if it were a fully researched theory. The same situation happens when adopting untested innovations.

Another key point about an innovation and its research is that the research must be closely aligned with the setting in which you plan to implement the innovation.

We have had very enlightening experiences that illustrate public schools' propensity for falling in love with innovations and adopting them without evidence of effectiveness—the research base. In our work in curriculum management auditing, we tally the number of new programs (innovations) in the district being audited. The following are our typical findings:

1. Innovations are adopted without asking about the research base; nearly all do not have a research base.

2. They are adopted throughout districts without being tested in a limited setting.

3. The goals are seldom defined, and when they are, they are not clear.

4. Their effects are not assessed after implementation.

5. There are too many of them for the district to monitor.

One astounding finding was in a very large city school system. The team of auditors found over 1,100 new programs—and none were being assessed for effectiveness and no one was monitoring them. The estimated cost was 15 million dollars. The known effects were zilch! This is not a good return in learning for dollars and time expended.

This is a good time in your reading to take a few minutes for reflection. In this reflective activity, outline your district's status versus its desired status in regard to Findings 1 through 5 listed above.

So what do you do before adopting an innovation? Here are a few steps to take to keep you moving in the right direction. When you see an innovation that you like, ask these questions:

1. What is the evidence that this innovation works? Is it published in a research journal?

Form 8.1

Existing Versus Desired Status (Write your reflections here.)	
Existing Status	**Desired Status**
1. Is an innovation's research base determined before being adopted?	
2. Are innovations tested on a small scale before being implemented widely?	
3. Are goals defined?	
4. Are effects assessed	
5. Is the total number of innovations manageable?	

2. Does this "solution" match a documented need in your school/district?

3. If the answers to 1 and 2 are yes, is the context of the site where you want to implement the innovation the same or nearly the same as the one in which the research was conducted?

If the answers to 1 through 3 are yes, give the innovation a try:

- Start on a small scale and check the evidence before proceeding.
- If revisions are needed, make them and try again.
- If your results are favorable, spread the practice, if desired, and continue to assess its effectiveness.
- If the results are not favorable and you see no promise in further trials, drop it!

So what do you do if the innovation matches a need in your school and it is well designed and makes a great deal of sense, but has no research base? The reality is that there are many apparently solid ideas that have no research base, and they won't have one until someone does the research—that is, until someone gives them a formal test. We know—this sounds too academic and time consuming, right? But the alternative is to waste massive quantities of teachers' and administrators' time and huge sums of money! Starting at one grade level in one school is a better alternative than investing massive resources in districtwide implementation. Many school districts have researchers who can help; if yours does not, check with a professor at your local university.

THE MBWA RESEARCH RESULTS

Now, let's get on with the purpose of this chapter—the research results. We have captured 10 highly desirable results of MBWA practices from the last 25 years of research literature. This is a very impressive list and provides a very firm foundation for making changes in administrator practice. Read on! Each of the nine outcomes is presented below, along with an explanation, and the tenth is presented in the next section of this chapter. But before you do read on, take a minute to predict (guess) what you think they may be, based on your professional experience. Be sure not to read ahead first!

Predictions of the Proven Beneficial Results of MBWA

(Write your predictions here.)

1. _____

2. _____

3. _____

4. _____

Let's start with the outcomes that are generally considered desirable and important. Remember that these are highly desirable and we think they are linked to the ultimate variable, or education's product—student learning. We call these proxy outcomes or variables, and a discussion of each follows.

1. Enhanced teacher satisfaction as defined by higher frequency of "flow" experiences (Frase, 2001; Galloway & Frase, 2003)

2. Improved teacher self-efficacy (Chester & Beaudin, 1996; Frase, 2001; Galloway & Frase, 2003)

3. Improved teacher attitudes toward professional development (Frase, 2001, 2003; Galloway & Frase, 2003)

4. Improved teacher attitudes toward teacher appraisal (Frase, 1998b, 2001; Galloway & Frase, 2003)

5. Increased perceived teacher efficacy of other teachers (Frase, 1998b, 2001; Galloway & Frase, 2003) and of the school (Frase, 2001; Galloway & Frase, 2003).

6. Improved classroom instruction (Freedman & LaFleur, 2003; Teddlie, Kirby, & Stringfield, 1989)

7. Improved teacher perception of principal effectiveness (Andrews & Soder, 1987; Freedman & LaFleur, 2002; Heck, Larsen, & Marcoulides, 1990; Sagor, 1992; Smith & Blase, 1991; Valentine, Clark, Nickerson, & Keefe, 1981; Wimpleberg, Teddlie, & Stringfield, 1989)

8. Improved student discipline and student acceptance of advice and criticism (Blase, 1987; Smith & Blase, 1991)

9. Improved teacher-perceived effectiveness of the school

This is a pretty impressive list! These are results that nearly everyone finds valuable. Each research result is discussed below. If you find that it gets deep, take a deep breath and try to hang in there. We hope you find it interesting.

1. Enhanced Teacher Satisfaction as Defined by Higher Frequency of "Flow" Experiences

So what is this *flow* stuff about? Well, it is really important. In this book and in the research, *flow is considered the most satisfying and motivating experience a person can have.* Flow experiences are periods of deep, intense involvement in activities that challenge but do not overwhelm one's skills. Csikszentmihalyi (1990) developed the theory and research.

Per his work and as interpreted by Whalen (1997), flow represents a distinct state of consciousness that integrates high but effortless concentration, intrinsic motivation, loss of awareness of self and time, facile response to challenge, and feelings of competence and freedom. Further, flow is the state in which people feel in control of their actions and feel a deep sense of exhilaration that becomes long cherished and a *landmark in memory for what life should be like* (p. 3).

Unfortunately, studies show that teachers in general, and inner-city teachers especially, are isolated in classrooms and receive little training that is helpful or valuable, little feedback on the quality of their work from others, and little assistance in helping them deal effectively with the many problems that confront them in their classrooms (Scholastic, Inc., 2000). Overall, teachers receive little assistance they can use to improve the quality of their work, according to Finn (as cited in Blair, 2000). As a partial result of these conditions, the past 20 years have shown a mass exodus of teachers from the profession and an all-time low level of morale (Farkas, Johnson, & Foleno, 2000).

One study (Frase, 2001) found that *frequency of principal classroom visits predicted increased frequency of teacher flow experiences*, or satisfaction. The practice of MBWA breaks teachers' feelings of isolation; also, when principals spend a lot of time in the classroom, they have a better idea of what the teachers' work is like and which obstacles need to be removed so that teachers can do their best work. *MBWA informs the principal and elicits strong ideas for feedback and assistance.* All of this adds up to a more highly motivated and more highly satisfied teacher.

The bottom-liners have a retort—they will say, "That's nice, but if it doesn't result in higher test scores, it doesn't matter." This response smacked one of us in the face a few years back during a presentation when someone in the audience spoke up, expressing his opinion about the value of flow. At the time it could not be said that flow had anything to do with learning—or test scores—but the belief was strongly held, and the research indicated that teacher motivation and satisfaction are important. A very bright doctoral student contacted one of us and said he wanted to do a dissertation on motivation and satisfaction. Well, that is a huge topic, so we introduced him to the literature and the research on flow, and he was fascinated by it—and how lucky for us! The results of his study are truly remarkable. We know that the frequency of principal classroom visits (MBWA) is positively related to a higher frequency of teacher flow experiences. Well, our doctoral student found that the *frequency of teacher flow experiences is directly connected to student cognition levels* (Zhu, 2001). He demonstrated that when teachers are experiencing flow, 25 percent more students are cognitively engaged in the lesson. So when naysayers tell you that teacher mental health doesn't matter, fill them in: MBWA yields increased frequency of teacher flow experiences, and these in turn yield higher levels of student cognition.

2. Improved Teacher Self-Efficacy

High teacher self-efficacy means this: The teacher believes strongly that he or she can perform the tasks (the instruction) required for the students to learn. The benefits of this are obvious. We definitely want and need teachers who believe strongly that they can produce learning. Ashton and Webb (1986) performed the seminal research demonstrating that teacher efficacy has a strong predictive link to student achievement. In their study, students of teachers with high self-efficacy levels consistently had higher achievement levels than students of teachers with lower self-efficacy levels. More recently, Goddard, Hoy, and Hoy (2000) found that collective teacher efficacy was positively associated with differences between schools in student-level achievement in both reading and mathematics.

So how does MBWA fit into this? The answer is easy: two studies—Chester and Beaudin (1996) and Frase (2001)—demonstrated that *MBWA behaviors are closely linked to higher teacher self-efficacy.* The Frase study showed that frequent classroom visits are linked to high teacher self-efficacy, and the Chester and Beaudin study showed that new teachers observed by their principal five times during the semester held higher efficacy beliefs than those not observed by their principal. The benefits of efficacy are clear, and so are the effects of MBWA on efficacy.

3. Improved Teacher Attitudes Toward Professional Development

Improving a teacher's ability to teach is obviously crucial to school success, and that is the purpose of professional development (PD). But the reality is that PD (inservice training) is generally considered a dismal failure across the nation. Teachers and experts overwhelmingly express little belief in the value of typical approaches to professional development (Culbertson, 1996; Fullan, 1995; Public Agenda Foundation, 1995). Annunziata (1997) characterized professional development as one-shot deals, superficial and faddish programs, feel-good sessions, make-and-take or bag-of-tricks content, and consultant-driven presentations. The National Staff Development Council asserted the opinion that current professional development practices are inadequately designed to serve as bridges that take teachers from where they are to where they need to be in order to better guide student learning (Culbertson, 1996). Further, Orlich, Remaley, and Facemyer (1993) found scant evidence that professional development is linked to student achievement; they also found that the evidence that did link professional development to increased student achievement was spurious due to use of inappropriate measurement techniques and research designs. Darling-Hammond and McLaughlin (1995) described professional development as crucial to educational success and offered guidelines for policy formation that would transform practices from the status quo to a robust enterprise that bene-fits students and teachers. Restated, there is a belief that professional development could result in increased student achievement, but that the policies for developing effective professional development practices and the research to support their efficacy are lacking.

The good news is that even without changing the structure of professional development offerings, *when principals are in classrooms more often, teachers express higher regard for professional development practices* (Frase, 2001).

4. Improved Teacher Attitudes Toward Teacher Appraisal

Improving teacher perceptions of the value of teacher appraisals is crucial, but unfortunately, the current value level matches that of pro-fessional development. Every state in the United States requires teacher and principal evaluations, and nearly all profess that the purpose of these evaluations is to improve instruction. It's clear that we have to do evaluations, and the purpose is fully legitimate—so we may as well do them, and we should do them well. This is not happening in the large majority of school districts. Teacher evaluation practices have been labeled deficient (Frase & Streshly, 1994; Haefele, 1993), chaotic (Medley, Coker, & Soar, 1984; Soar, Medley, & Coker, 1983), inadequate (Scriven, 1981), of little value in assisting teachers in improving class-room instruction (Duke, 1995; Frase & Streshly, 1994, 2000; Nevo, 1994), and unjust in consideration of the extraordinary cost (Scriven, 1988). Moreover, principal training in effective supervision and profes-sional development practices is generally shown to be absent, grossly ineffective, or divorced from teacher evaluations (Annunziata, 1997; Duke, 1995; Haefele, 1993). This remains the case in spite of the general agreement that these areas must be intertwined (Annunziata, 1997; Scriven, 1967). Teachers also hold teacher appraisal in low esteem (Frase & Streshly, 1994).

Well, that is a pretty bleak view! But our guess is that most educa-tors already know that teacher evaluations, as currently practiced, are a waste of time. So what does all of this mean? It means that we must do a better job. The good news is that *those teachers whose principals are in classrooms frequently and focus on curriculum and instruction hold the teacher appraisal process in higher regard than other teachers* (Frase, 1998b, 2001). The requirement that schools conduct teacher evaluations is not going to go away, nor should it. We need to do a better job in this area, and a great place to start is by being in classrooms much more frequently, finding out about curriculum, instruction, and the obstacles that confront teachers.

5. Increased Perceived Teacher Efficacy of Other Teachers and of the School

The research-proven value of higher levels of teachers' perceived efficacy of other teachers and of the school is just breaking through, but so far the results are impressive. For instance, Goddard et al. (2000) found that collective teacher efficacy (the efficacy level of the teaching staff as a whole) is positively associated with student achievement in reading and mathematics. The importance of this outcome is also supported by Morton Deutsch's (1949) work on social interdependence. In his theory and research, he found that groups have greater success when the individuals in the group perceive that others in the group can also reach their goals. This is similar to Kurt Lewin's (1952; Katz & Kahn, 1966) belief that the whole is greater than the sum of the parts applies to the concept of teamwork.

The benefit of this finding is clear: *As belief in the efficacy of others increases, so does the school's attainment of its goals.* Certainly teachers are much more likely to pursue the school's mission with greater enthusiasm when they believe others are capable of carrying a fair share of the load.

The good news here is that research is showing that the frequency of principal classroom visits is strongly associated with higher teacher-perceived efficacy of other teachers and the school. Just as with self-efficacy, we want to hire teachers who believe that their fellow teachers and the school can do the job that needs to be done.

So when we get into these psychological areas of education, how do we go about making progress? When it comes to MBWA, the answer is relatively easy and does not require the skills of a clinical psychologist. We know that *MBWA, particularly being in classrooms frequently, increases teachers' perceived efficacy levels of other teachers* (Frase, 1998b, 2001) *and the school* (Frase, 2001). The caution should be against thinking that going into classrooms will make everything good and well. Only magic and divine intervention could do that.

6. Improved Classroom Instruction

High-quality instruction results in higher levels of student achievement than does poor-quality instruction. This relationship is like a blinding flash of the obvious. The good news is that we now have a strong research base for knowing this absolutely (Marzano, 2001; Tileston, 2000). The other good news is that we have strong evidence that higher frequency of principal classroom visits and constant focus on curriculum and instruction are positively related to improved classroom instruction (Teddlie et al., 1989). Will more frequent classroom visits make all teachers great teachers? No! But it is a step in the right direction.

7. Improved Teacher Perception of Principal Effectiveness

Andrews and Soder (1987); Heck et al. (1990); Sagor (1992); Smith and Blase (1991); Valentine, Clark, Nickerson, and Keefe (1981); and Wimpleberg et al. (1989) all found that *as the frequency of the principal's classroom visits increased, so did teachers' perception of the principal's effectiveness.*

This is a great outcome in that it just flat-out makes principals feel good! Principals want to believe that teachers think of them as effective, which no doubt enhances self-worth. This outcome is linked to the collective efficacy finding of Goddard et al. (2000): When we believe we can, we try and we do—successfully.

8. Improved Student Discipline and Student Acceptance of Advice and Criticism

Every vice principal in charge of discipline will love this section. The discipline job is a tough one, and it seems that it never ends. The percentage of repeat offenders is depressing. The good news with Blase's (1987) and Smith and Blase's (1991) work is that *being more visible and being in classrooms more often is positively related to improved discipline and acceptance of advice!* When we reflect on the number and severity of discipline cases in some schools, this outcome offers great potential and hope.

9. Improved Teacher-Perceived Effectiveness of the School

This is also, in some respects, a feel-good finding. Really, it is nice when teachers believe their school is effective. It leads to higher self-esteem, pride, and confidence.

Constant focus on curriculum and instruction and being in classrooms frequently leads to this common goal. The key here is that *teachers have higher perceived levels of school success when the principals are in their classrooms frequently* (Frase, 2001).

Now, let's take a look at the research conducted thus far on the walk-through process described in this book.

THE WALK-THROUGH WITH REFLECTIVE QUESTION RESEARCH

The first research study focusing on our walk-through process with reflective questions has been completed and the results are very favorable (Freedman & LaFleur, 2003). This work focused on interviews with principals in two school districts. All of the principals had experienced the formal Level 1, two-day walk-through training. Freedman's qualitative analysis found the following themes:

- Develops focus on curriculum
- Increases visibility in classrooms
- Stimulates rethinking of the principal's role
- Clarifies and helps overcome time and politics as reform obstacles
- Further develops positive school culture
- Enhances comfort level with reflective questions

The first bullet is exceptionally desirable. As you have read in this book, deep alignment of the written, taught, and tested curriculum is absolutely necessary to ensure that children excel, and assessing whether what is being taught aligns with the written curriculum is the principal's primary purpose when making a walk-through. After walk-through training, principals volunteered that they were much more attuned to the curriculum being taught. This is a huge outcome. It indicates that walk-through training has profound effects.

The second major research project (Gray & Frase, 2003) on walk-throughs with reflective feedback is nearing completion. This project includes quantitative analyses of survey results and qualitative analyses of 27 teachers and principals. The initial findings are also very positive.

So, that is a lot of information. Let's take a few minutes to think about it. This is a good time to work with a team or partner. What do you see in these findings? How will they affect your administrative practices? Use the form below to list your ideas.

Your Administrative Practices

(Write your ideas here.)

What do you see in these findings?

_____

_____

_____

_____

How will they affect your administrative practices?

_____

_____

_____

We now know that MBWA, primarily frequent classroom visits and being visible in the school, leads to many highly desirable outcomes. The next question is, so what? What impact does it directly have on student learning? Well, here is the homerun, the 105-yard touchdown—the ultimate variable—the coup de grace. What impact does principal MBWA have on student learning? Here it is, outcome number 10: *MBWA increases student learning across socioeconomic and cultural lines!*

That is powerful. It is the "beef." We want students to learn: That is why we are in education. These results are absolutely great news. And it is very interesting to note that MBWA behaviors affect student achievement across all socioeconomic levels, but they have the greatest impact on the students who need it most—those who come from low-socioeconomic status (SES) homes. In fact, there are few factors that result in higher achievement for students from low-SES backgrounds. MBWA does accomplish this feat, and the research base to support this is broad and deep (Andrews & Soder, 1987; Andrews, Soder, & Jacoby, 1986; Hallinger & Heck, 1996; Heck, 1991, 1992).

So there you have it. MBWA has a very strong research base. Although the letters "MBWA" may sound a bit whimsical, the practices they represent are as sound as a concrete pylon.

Again, this is a lot of information to assimilate. Let's take time to settle back and think about this last research finding dealing with student achievement. What are your thoughts about it? And what changes might you want to make in your administrative practices because of it?

(Use this space for recording your thoughts about student learning and MBWA.)

My thoughts are:

1. _____

2. _____

3. _____

4. _____

How this might impact my administrative practices:

_____

_____

_____

_____

That pretty much does it for this chapter. You have been very patient in enduring what some people may call *boring* stuff. If it has gotten just too heavy, consider Woody Allen's advice on what causes success: "Eighty percent of life depends on *showing up*"—and the other 20 percent is being on time! That's MBWA.

Let's summarize this chapter. You have learned about the following:

1. Faddism and the carte blanche adoption of innovations in American schools without evidence of effectiveness

2. How many schools and districts fall subject to faddism, accepting unworthy innovations

3. Steps to use when considering adopting an innovation in your school/district—how to avoid faddism

4. The background and history of MBWA, including stories from ancient history and modern-day administrative practices

5. The necessity of a research and theory base

6. The MBWA research base—the 10 highly desirable outcomes, including *improved student learning*

If any of these seem vague to you, take a minute and go back and review. Next let's think about the chapter in it entirety. Use the box below.

What impressed you most in this chapter?	How do you feel about these ideas?
1. _____	1. _____
2. _____	2. _____
3. _____	3. _____
4. _____	4. _____
5. _____	5. _____
6. _____	6. _____

Understanding the Walk-Through as a Discursive Practice

O ur walk-through model may be described as a *discursive practice.* This term comes from postmodern analytical thinking in which all forms of communication are examined critically. A *discourse* such as the one that might take place between the principal and a teacher is not only a way of representing a world, but also a way of actively constructing that world and deriving meaning from its implementation (Fairclough, 1992). Any given discourse does three things:

1. It creates "social identities" and uses frames of communication to position its subjects within the communication.

2. It creates social relationships between people.

3. It contributes to the construction of knowledge and belief. (Fairclough, 1992)

Professional practice occurs within already existing systems of belief (called ideologies), power structures, and social structures. Language about professional practices can be neither neutral nor independent of these structures. Rather, language use is necessarily subject to a process of continual exchange and transformation, and language use is negotiated within spoken and unspoken rules (see Fairclough, 1992). We should be mindful of how our language impacts the meaning of what we say and provides boundaries for that meaning. This is especially true when we are trying to use that language to change relationships and create a different culture in schools.

This Downey Walk-Through is more than a model of adult-to-adult supervision. In fact, it does not involve supervision in the traditional sense of the word. Rather, it is a relationship between two professionals: one a classroom teacher, and the other, the school principal or other administrative officer. This relationship is seen as collegial, that is, a pairing of professional equals, though the bureaucratic positioning may signify otherwise. As stated in Chapter 7, we like to think of it as collaborative, reflective culture.

Professional practice regarding supervision as implemented in most school settings establishes an unequal relationship between the principals and teachers. The traditional *discursive practice* of supervision reinforces hierarchical relationships. The social identities of the principal and the teacher are constructed on clear boundaries of authority and assumptions about power within a social structure, which in turn shapes and is shaped by these social identities.

The traditional social identities of principals and teachers are shown in Figure 9.1. The figure indicates the usual hierarchical interaction that occurs within a legalistic and bureaucratic social structure. The current *discursive practice* of exchange between principals and teachers consistently reinforces itself. The act of supervision, which is based on *observation*, assumes a specific form. The traditional observation by the principal is itself an exercise of power in the process of gathering knowledge. Information gained by observation is used to reinforce a hierarchical relationship in which the teacher is continually reminded of the principal's superior position, because the principal has the legal authority to engage in a specific form of compliance review that is central to institutional authority and functioning.

The principal's observation is a kind of "institutional gaze" that is peculiarly normative; that is, the principal's gaze is often transformed into evaluation commentary that is placed in categories (often on checklists). A normative gaze is primarily an exercise in determining compliance; it is, at its core, *disciplinary*. A normative gaze that is centered on disciplinary determinations is corrective, sometimes punitive, or occasionally therapeutic, but it cannot be liberating or transformational. These responses would seriously threaten the *discursive practice* itself.

Traditional supervision is shaped by, and in turn reinforces, not only a bureaucratic social environment, but also the content and form of all professional discourse within a school's structure. The earmarks of a bureaucracy are the following:

- The presence of differentiated roles that are arranged in hierarchical fashion (superior/subordinate)

Figure 9.1   Pyramidal Bureaucratic Structure in Which the Principal-Teacher
Relationship is Embedded

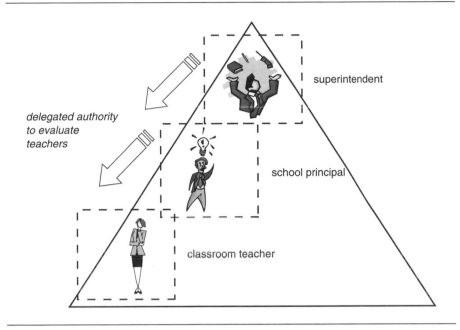

- Job descriptions and pay scales that correspond to the hierarchical roles
- Job/role authority rooted in the law (a legal basis for authority)
- Roles/jobs attached to tasks that are related to broader organizational or organizational subunits

As stated before, our model changes the language of exchange between principals and teachers. This alteration not only reflects a different purpose for a classroom observation, but a different relationship between principals and teachers.

The model changes the role relationship between teachers and principals via the *reflective question.* A reflective question between the principal and the teacher in which there is no one correct answer means that this is an exchange between equals. The principal is not playing "gotcha" and not doing a "discrepancy analysis" with a checklist. As the principal and teacher work through their conversation together, a dialogue that can take many weeks, the exchange is marked by the following qualities:

- An exploration of alternatives and varying modes of response
- An explication of classroom context and how this variable may influence decision making

- Students serving as forms and foci of information in which instructional practices may be grounded
- Consideration of the types and the nature of objectives the teacher is attempting to accomplish

As the conversation continues, the relationship evolves from a bureaucratic, legalistic one to that of two or more professionals in mutual pursuit of critical reflection regarding current practice. That conversation is pictured in Figure 9.2. It illustrates how the relationship of a principal and a teacher engaging in a true conversation involving critical reflection *de-bureaucratizes* schools by changing the anchor for the superior/subordinate relationship. By abolishing the axis of control as the primary locus for evaluation and shifting it to development, a new dialogic model of professional work is created.

The walk-through therefore consists of two broad thrusts. The first is the technical acquisition of the skills and philosophy of the walk-through process. That involves structured observation within a time-framed application. The second thrust involves the use of the reflective question(s) as part of an ongoing conversation. The reflective question is generated by the data gathered in the structured observation. By re-centering the nature of the follow-up, the positional base of both the teacher and principal is equalized and becomes collegial. Stretched over many teachers, the school climate is altered one teacher at a time.

Figure 9.2 How the Downey Approach Changes the Professional Relationship

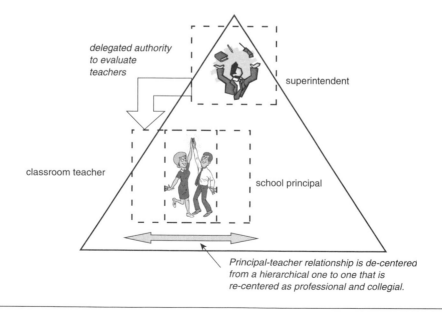

delegated authority to evaluate teachers

superintendent

classroom teacher

school principal

Principal-teacher relationship is de-centered from a hierarchical one to one that is re-centered as professional and collegial.

EXAMINING THE DIMENSIONS
OF THE WALK-THROUGH

One way to examine the nature of the first part of the walk-through is shown in Figure 9.3. The most common form of evaluation/supervision is the checklist approach where the principal spends some time in the classroom. That method ideally fits a bureaucratic structure. It reinforces the principal's role as "the boss," and the checklist becomes the method of control exercised over teachers to compel conformance to the items on the evaluation. A checklist represents "generalized and itemized behaviors," which have been abstracted from any specific context to be applicable in multiple contexts. Thus, the traditional approach to evaluation and supervision is superficial to any specific context. A slightly improved approach would have a high interpersonal dimension using a checklist.

However, checklists have inherent disadvantages. They are based on assumptions, not the least of which is that specific objectives do not make much of a difference in most approaches. Checklists epitomize the "normative gaze" of the administrator. When observation is defined by the need for the normative gaze, classroom walk-throughs become primarily *disciplinary* and focused on the need for "corrections."

Clinical supervision is much more contextualized; however, it does not fundamentally change the principal/teacher relationship. It is still the principal who is the initiator and the person who "writes up" the extended

Figure 9.3   Two-Dimensional Representation of the Downey Model
Compared to Alternatives Such as Traditional Evaluation and
Clinical Supervision

	Collegiality	
	Low	High
Low	Formal evaluation with checklist	Humane approach with strong human relations with checklists
High	Clinical supervision	Downey Walk-through

(left axis label: Context specificity — Low / High)

record. So, while clinical supervision is more personalized and contextualized, it is still an exercise in bureaucratic control completed within pyramidal organizational lines and it does not alter those lines. There is nothing in the approach to clinical supervision that creates a more collegial climate in a school or that moves the interaction between principals and teachers away from a disciplinary or normative focus.

Contrast this with the Downey model that, through the reflective-questioning technique, does change that relationship. It is classroom specific and therefore offers a highly contextualized and personal interaction between principals and teachers. This occurs if both thrusts of the model are utilized, not simply the walk-through technique alone, but a walk-through that is centered in the reflective conversation between principal and teachers, and is therefore moving toward de-centering the disciplinary nature of classroom observation and the necessity of engaging in "corrections" based on normative assumptions.

CHANGING THE DISCURSIVE PRACTICE OF "CORRECTIVE" SUPERVISION

The dimensions of the change in the discursive practice of supervision are shown in Table 9.1. Research conducted by Freedman and LaFleur (2003) and others supports many of the changes described in their interviews of principals and other administrators who have learned how to do classroom walk-throughs.

Table 9.1   The Changed Axes of Professional Practice in the Downey Model of Classroom Walk-Throughs

From	*To*
• The teacher as a subordinate worker, a child in a dependent relationship with authority figures	• The teacher as a colleague, an adult with autonomy to make decisions about how to construct the work and execute it in the work setting
• Three or four formal, infrequent, lengthy observations and evaluations per year, dependent on checklists and forms—followed up with a scheduled, formal appointment with the evaluator • Evaluations becoming part of the "permanent file"	• Many informal observations, interactions, and visitations per year which are paperless and conversational • Discussions with the principal are held in informal and unscheduled places and times; may later become formal if necessary

From	To
	• Do not become part of the "permanent file"
• Teachers evaluated on checklists that rest on abstracted practices that are "context free" and "out of curriculum"	• Teachers are observed in specific contexts, relative to specific curricular objectives they are attempting to teach
• Effectiveness is considered generic and rated in the abstract without reference to specific curricular objectives and specific instructional settings, and performance is considered outside of any relationships with the supervisor, colleagues, students, and parents	• Effective practices are contingent upon specific classes with specific students in specific settings
	• Effectiveness is relational and situated in specific contexts
	• Performance is viewed as being within a constellation of other humans in the work setting
• Principals look for conformance to abstracted lists of generalized instructional practices and techniques that are oblivious to specific curricular objectives and interested only in the "discrepancies" or gaps	• Principals first look at the objectives the teacher is trying to accomplish and how the objectives are manifested in the specific pedagogical decisions made by the teacher in a specific classroom setting
• These are the "gotcha" glitches that are often the gist of "recommendations" for improvements that change little and do not lead to improvement in student achievement	• Effective classroom practice is contextually defined by the content of the objectives, which forms the relational borders in which the teacher and the students interact
• Abstracted lists of "proficiencies" that are essentially curriculum free have little to do with learning specific curricular objectives	• The principal is not looking for breakdowns in abstracted lists of teacher proficiencies, but for the connection between pedagogical decisions and the linkage to specific curricular content to be learned
• This dominant approach to classroom supervision focuses on the wrong things. It is best captured in the phrase, "The operation was a success but the patient died"	• This relationship is the "hub" of viewing what is going on in the classroom and it is where the principal begins the conversation with a teacher about his or her design and delivery of the curriculum in a specific classroom setting
	• Achievement is defined by what students learn, not conformance to context-free abstractions of "good teaching"

(Continued)

Table 9.1 (Continued)

From	To
	• The principal is foremost concerned with the locus of the decisions made by the teacher and not so much with in any one specific outcome
• Classroom practice is confined to the classroom	• Classroom practice is influenced by the climate and culture of the entire school
	• No classroom is isolated from the rest of the school
	• Effective teaching practice is relational and never permanent
	• It exists within a network and it must be a constant process of interaction on an adult-to-adult model of conversation

SOME ISSUES WITH THE MODEL

1. Assuming That the Model Is Only a Technical Approach

A superficial view of the model is that it is simply a way to shorten the time requirements to perform full classroom observations and reduce them to new checklists. The model can be adapted to fit the current bureaucratic *discursive practice* by reducing the major points to a checklist. This approach compromises the full power of the Downey perspective by trading away the changes in the principal-teacher relationship to reinforce the customary disciplinary purpose of classroom observation. The administrator who does this is not interested in the establishment of a more collegial and empowering discourse about classroom practice *with* teachers, and may see a change in the relationship with teachers as threatening to his or her power base. This is unfortunate. No change in classroom observation technique is likely to improve the current *discursive practice* for this administrator.

2. Being Unaware That One's Perspective Is Still the Normative Gaze

Seasoned administrators may find it terribly difficult to change the internal lenses through which they examine classroom practices. The normative gaze centered on disciplinary conformance is usually bound up with the roles themselves as they have come to be defined. Principals "do" this and "don't do" that. Principals are expected to "correct" things, to be "in charge," and to ask corrective questions and expect "answers".

Teachers, too, have come to expect certain kinds of questions from principals. These questions require answers, not reflection. And the answers are more or less "right" or "wrong." So teachers may carry in their heads role expectations grounded in the extant *discursive practice.* Should a principal try the new approach grounded in the idea that there is no "right" answer but an array of possible answers, teachers may feel the principal doesn't really know what is expected, or that he or she is fishing for something they may feel anxious about. Teachers used to a former principal who was exceptionally corrective and prescriptive and who have adapted to such procedures, may come to see a new principal functioning from a different view as "weak."

Much of the newly developed state accountability systems of student achievement and teacher/administrator evaluation are inspection oriented and can lead to punitive sanctions for teachers and administrators. Such systems work against collegiality and professional growth that is empowering and liberating. They are conformance-dominated models designed to ensure uniformity and standardization of classroom practices.

Our approach places at its center the autonomy of the classroom teacher as a purposeful practitioner engaged in critical, professional reflective practice. Such purposeful actions involve questioning the wisdom of system-designed rules that may limit teacher effectiveness and, ultimately, student learning. Students cannot learn the benefits of democratic life if their teachers are pawns in a faceless and impersonal machine.

3. Being Unable to See That Change Is a Process and Not an Outcome

Principals tackling the kinds of changes inherent in the model need to think about change as a process and not a place or an outcome. The model can be approached in stages. However, it is a process and not a place. One does not travel from the status quo to some other place and quit. The model involves a process of exchange and interaction that is a "way of life" in a school that is becoming better and better over time.

Table 9.2 identifies the important generic stages or periods in the implementation of the Downey model of classroom observation.

Do not think of these stages as perfectly linear, and bear in mind that it is possible to be at one stage and revert to a former stage if external or

Table 9.2   Stages In the Implementation Process of the Downey Curriculum
Walk-Through

Stage	Characteristics
1. Introductory Stage	**Initial Awkwardness/Tension**
The principal begins using the walk-through methodology in a school where the staff has been used to the traditional, normative, and "corrective" approach to classroom observation with traditional follow-up activities.	Teachers may react defensively, feel uncomfortable with frequent visitations that do not lead to expected outcomes such as formal notes or checklist observations.
2. Preliminary Comfort Stage	**Growing Awareness and Acceptance**
The principal continues to use the walk-through as designed—refusing to engage in "correct" feedback and focusing on reflective questions.	As the principal continues to use the approach and explain why he or she does some things and not others, there is an increasing awareness and acceptance of the approach.
3. Climate Change Stage	**Wider Conversations and Discourse Shift**
As more and more teachers become involved in reflective questioning and thinking about classroom practice, teachers begin talking with one another about instruction in their classrooms. The nature of the professional discourse begins to shift.	As more and more teachers become used to the new model they begin to seek increased number of ways to grow and undertake advanced application of classroom practices, some of which may challenge state-imposed norms and may involve some work by the principal to sharpen teachers' questions and focus.
4. A New Discursive Practice Stage	**Increasing Distance From the Old Methods and Normative, Correct Viewpoints**
The principal has created a new discursive practice on a schoolwide basis toward classroom observation and discussions about what is going on in classrooms at all levels. This stage is marked by a near total break with bureaucratic procedures and expectations regarding classroom evaluation.	The school has shifted to a new and more divergent perspective about classroom practice. Teachers themselves begin to take on roles with one another that formerly would have been pursued only by the principal.

internal forces change. For example, suppose several teachers at a school retire. In this school district, due to provisions in the union contract, teachers can transfer into the school from other schools with their seniority intact. These transferred teachers are not used to the walk-through and may initially be resistant, especially to unannounced visitations. The principal may be hit with some grievances that may seek to limit visitations to formal and announced times only. The school may have been at Stage 3, the climate change stage. Because of these staffing changes, the school may revert to Stage 2, the preliminary comfort stage, or even to Stage 1.

It should be obvious that the principal needs to be communicating to teachers the purpose of the walk-through. The principal should build understanding with teachers as to the purpose of many short, unannounced classroom visitations as opposed to the required one or two full-length classroom visitations with which most teachers are familiar. The principal must ensure that teachers do not see an increase in the frequency of visitations as a clue that "something is wrong," or that the principal is applying pressure of some sort in a new model of "close supervision." Remember that most teachers have never had a collegial relationship with a principal, and nearly all will be unfamiliar with the *reflective question* as the basis of a relationship with a supervisor.

If there is some stumbling around in trying to forge a new professional relationship between principals and teachers, it may in part be due to the inexperience of the school principal with the process, especially with the reflective question. Principals must work hard not to fall back into the old "corrective" model of supervision, even as they experiment with the reflective question. Principals should try to verbalize the expected changes with teachers as they work at reframing their relationships with them. Teachers will have to be reassured that the principal is not going to offer "corrective" statements or "disciplinary suggestions" in order to calm them, that the principal is not "playing games."

Due to bureaucratic and other legal requirements, the principal may not be able to completely shed the trappings of the older, more corrective and discipline-centered form of observation. This requirement presents the situation in which the principal is trying to move the school into a professional, adult-to-adult model of collegiality, at the same time that the older evaluation system functions on an adult-to-child relationship, which is corrective in nature. Principals will have to work with teachers so that they understand how the nature of evaluation and classroom observation is intimately connected to more basic assumptions about the larger *discursive practice* in which each is enmeshed and mutually reinforcing.

The basic message here is *don't just start doing walk-throughs and expect teachers to figure out what's happening.* Take time to explain what you are doing, the assumptions behind your actions, and where you expect the process to lead. Engage teachers as professional partners in helping you realize the goals of the walk-through process.

Still another facet to consider in implementing the walk-through process will be the response of your own supervisors. If your "boss" believes that only the older, disciplinary, and correction-based approach is appropriate, you must consider carefully the reactions to changing the process without first having a serious discussion with your boss. To ground your discussion, it is recommended that you use Table 9.1, titled *The Changed Axes of Professional Practice in the Downey Model of Classroom Walk-Throughs.* This table can serve to provide talking points for you to use in a conversation with your superior in which you describe the big picture and illustrate that the walk-through is not merely a technical alteration, but a substantive change in philosophy and focus for school improvement.

A PAUSE TO CONSIDER YOUR SPECIFIC SITUATION

Take a few moments to consider the situation in your own school. Think about the following questions:

1. How bureaucratic is your school? Are the traditional roles present? Are they heavily reinforced and observed? What is the current comfort level with the current situation?

2. If you are the principal in the school and you are new, what were the habits of the previous principal regarding observation and evaluation? Were teachers comfortable with them?

3. If you are a seasoned principal at the same school, how do you think your teachers will react to the new approach? What actions can you take prior to initiating the walk-through process to ensure it will be received positively?

4. How much does the walk-through process deviate from the traditional methods employed at your school, and in what ways will the older model detract from the goals of the newer one?

5. How will your supervisors react to doing observation and evaluation differently? Do your own supervisors understand the difference?

TROUBLESHOOTING PROBLEMS WITH THE DOWNEY WALK-THROUGH

This section is designed to point out responses to a variety of issues that may arise as the reader engages in an implementation of the Downey Walk-Through process. It is not designed to be exhaustive. The issues are *framed* within the generic stages of implementation in Table 9.2.

1. Issues in the Generic Stage 1: Introductory Stage

Lack of Teacher Buy-In or Deeper Understanding of the Process

QUESTION: The teachers don't seem to be "buying in" to the process. I've tried explaining it, but they just don't seem to be getting it. Some of my really good teachers want me to "write up" my observations as with the old evaluation system.

ANSWER: If you are an experienced principal at a school where you enjoy some tenure, remember that observation and evaluation occur within a *discursive practice* as described in this chapter. A *discursive practice* creates social relationships between people and it positions people within those relationships. Teachers need to see that the new walk-through approach *enhances* their position within the school, that is, it elevates them to a new relationship with you, the principal. You must be sure that they understand that you *also* want a different relationship with them. Perhaps you have only explained the technical issues and differences of the walk-through process and they do not see that the social relationships will also change. Your comfort level is communicated along with your intellectual understanding of the process. You communicate at both levels, cognitive and emotional. Reexamine your own feelings. Are you ready for a change in relationships?

2. Issues in Generic Stage 2: Preliminary Comfort Stage

The Lack of an Adequate Curriculum

QUESTION: The curriculum in my district is either nonexistent or not helpful to me in conducting classroom walk-throughs. I have no idea what I should be looking for in areas in which the state has no expectations or test protocols. For example, when I visit the art teacher, I have no idea what the objectives should be. I have the same problem with some other areas of the curriculum. What can I do?

ANSWER: This is a fairly common problem and may be an issue in Stage 1 as well. Most states and many provinces in Canada have developed curricular frameworks. That is usually a good place to start. Many states and provinces have also created more specific lists of performance indicators, which can begin to serve the function of guideposts for various levels. In most cases, even these will have to be broken down into more specific and discrete units to really become functional in the walk-through process. You can use the walk-through process as a way to get teachers and your district-level curriculum consultants to see the importance of developing greater specificity in their curriculum documents. In the absence of any other guidance on this issue, you can begin to look at the continuity and specificity that may be contained in your textbook adoption list, if there is an element common to them across grade levels.

3. Issues in Generic Stage 3: Climate Change

The Problem of Teacher Isolates

QUESTION: The school's overall climate has changed. We are more collegial and there is even discussion in the teacher's lounge about classroom dynamics. However, some teachers have not participated in this change. They are becoming more and more isolated. They don't seem willing or even comfortable in talking about what they do in their classroom. Most of them are the more senior faculty. They like the "old way" where everybody did their own thing. As the momentum picks up, these faculty members' apathy is becoming more noticeable. What can be done to change their attitudes and have them join the conversation?

ANSWER: Some teachers may not join in the changes because they feel to do so would mean a loss of their autonomy or control within their own workplace. Others may lack the conceptual framework or even the vocabulary involved with it. Still others may have a very different way of describing their work environment than the language permits. It is usually true that the walk-through process has been initiated within the broader mainstream of state-imposed accountability schemes. Teachers may be resistant to engage in any method or process that appears to be part and parcel of these accountability schemes, especially if principals have embraced forms of disciplinary punishment and negative visibility (such as publishing test scores by teacher). Instead of seeing teacher resistance in this situation as a hindrance, view the teacher's reluctance as a healthy manifestation of the desire to retain autonomy and independence, a key to professionalism. The Downey Walk-Through approach recognizes the primacy of teacher independence and utilizes an interaction pattern in which the teacher may be elevated to peer status with the principal. If the content of the walk-through is centered solely on the state or district's tested curriculum, it is easy for teachers to see this kind of walk-through as concerned only with test scores. As such, it is simply another form of participatory "monitoring." The key person in this process is the principal and how he or she sees the so-called reluctant teacher. We are so used to deficit models in schooling evaluation that it may be convenient to see this teacher as lacking in some respect. While the lack of skills or technical language may be the reason for reluctance in some cases, in others teacher resistance is not a deficit at all. Principals must be knowledgeable of how and when teachers should be engaged in reflective dialogue, and use the walk-through technique to open up conversations with all teachers.

4. Issues in Generic Stage 4: A New Discursive Practice

The Problem of a Clash of Evaluative Narratives

QUESTION: As my staff has become more and more used to the walk-through process and its emphasis on reflective questions, there is more and more resistance to using the older and district-required correction-based model. This model is also embedded in the teachers union's contract and is referenced in many ways, especially if problems have been identified on the evaluative checklist. Many of my best teachers want to abandon this older method and employ the walk-through methodology. What should I do?

ANSWER: First, view this development as a healthy and desired state and make sure that your teachers are not punished for expressing their viewpoints. Explore with your central office personnel administrator the option of simply writing up the conversation you have been having with your teachers that is inspired by the reflective questions. If this is possible, the situation would provide a wonderful opportunity for you and each teacher to finally put to paper what your conversation has been about over several weeks or months. If necessary, you can complete the required checklist with each teacher and attach the amendments of the reflective questions. For teachers who have not participated, you simply use the required checklist as before.

SUMMARY

This chapter has been about the "big picture" of conducting the Downey Walk-Through. Inevitably, the big picture is theoretical. We have proposed that the theoretical framework is that of *discourse theory* (see Fairclough, 1992) based on the work of Michael Foucault (1972). *Discourse theory* is not only about communication, but also about structure and social identities. The Downey Walk-Through process is about changing the current disciplinary (or norm-centered), correction-based evaluative process to a more collegial, peer-to-peer practice of engaging in conversation about professional practices. While it involves some technical skills, these are centered in a very different notion of observing classroom activities, as this book has been describing.

Linking the Walk-Through Process to a Model of Teacher Growth

In this closing chapter, we will show how the walk-through process can be combined with a teacher growth model to enhance and deepen reflective dialogue. The phases of a teacher growth model will be described with specific suggestions for how the varied levels of reflective discourse can best be used with teachers at different phases of the model. The concept of reflection is fundamental to both the walk-through model and the teacher growth model, and we will trace the development of the concept from Dewey to more sophisticated models of adult learning such as transformational learning. This discussion should enable the reader to discover how to deepen and expand rich opportunities for professional growth.

We see the walk-through process as a form of differentiated professional development. The typical approach to formalized professional development today is based on the assumption that there is one set of procedures that works for all teachers (see Marczely, 2001). This is simply not the case. Professional development that is effective for the beginning teacher is far different from that which is effective for teachers at other points in their careers. The walk-through process lends itself to these differing needs.

Take a few minutes to reflect on the type of professional development that has been most effective for you during your career.

- As a beginning teacher, did you find that you needed someone to talk to about instructional practice? Who filled that role for you?
- How would you describe those conversations? What was your role, and what was the role of the person you were talking to?

- Did mutual trust and respect impact those conversations? In what way?
- As you gained experience in the classroom over several years, did you still seek out someone you felt comfortable with to dialogue about your role as a professional educator?
- Did the nature of those conversations change over time? If so, how?
- When do you have the most meaningful conversations about practice now? With whom? What role does your school principal play in these conversations?

REFLECTION

Reflections on How Meaningful Conversations

About Practice Change Over Time

(Write your comments here.)

_____

_____

_____

_____

WALK-THROUGHS AND THE TEACHER GROWTH MODEL

A teacher growth model that is highly compatible with the walk-through evolved over time and is detailed in the book, *The Life Cycle of the Career Teacher Model* (Steffy, 1989; Steffy & Wolfe, 1997; Steffy, Wolfe, Pasch, & Enz, 2000). This model provides a framework for creating a professional learning environment to support continued growth and development of teachers over a lifetime career. We see the walk-through process as a mechanism for the implementation of this model.

The model is developmental because it proposes and describes an ongoing process that takes place throughout a teaching career. In

common with other developmental theories, the model views personal/
professional growth as unfolding through interactions between individuals
and their environments in an identifiable, sequential pattern; acknowledges that individuals move along the continuum at different rates; and
views the growing individual as an active participant in his or her own
development.

The model posits phases of development in common with Erikson
(1968), Levinson, Darrow, Klein, Levinson, and McKee (1978); and others.
Phase theories tend to focus on content and tasks that flow from one to
another along a continuum. In contrast, stage theories, such as those of
Piaget (1954), Loevinger (1987), and others, focus more on structure and
organization and typically describe more discrete relationships.

In the life cycle model, each of the six phases is content and task
specific and exists along the continuum of excellent teaching. The model
presents a vision of good practice based on transferring knowledge and
contextual experience to another phase. As in real life, development and
transformation are blurred. The strength of this model is its focus on the
processes of how one continues to grow and become more competent. The
model is grounded in transformative learning theory.

The process of reflection and renewal is the central, critical aspect of this
model. As Bell and Gilbert (1996) noted, "Reflection is a skill which is inher-
ently part of constructivism, particularly personal constructivism." Reflection
must be purposeful for teachers to construct meaning for themselves.

If teachers are not successful in attaining personal and professional
growth via reflective activities, they enter a negative, downward spiral. In
the model this is referred to as withdrawal, and it marks a period in which
teachers are unsuccessful in their efforts to remain engaged and growth
oriented. The progression from initial withdrawal to persistent withdrawal
and finally to deep withdrawal involves increasingly negative responses
in three key areas: physical, emotional, and mental processes (Pines,
Aronson, & Kafrey, 1981).

The model also connects personal and reflective development
and growth to specific external factors such as reactions/responses to
conflict, changing social contexts, and the impact of school cultures;
larger community and societal pressures also play a critical fulcrum and
balancing force role.

THE MODEL

The Life Cycle of the Career Teacher model (Steffy & Wolfe, 1997; Steffy
et al., 2000) is based on the premise that, given the appropriate learning

environment, teachers will continue to grow and develop throughout their professional lifetime, thus achieving the goal of the National Commission on Teaching and America's Future (NCTAF) (1996). The model identifies six phases of development: Novice, Apprentice, Professional, Expert, Distinguished, and Emeritus (see Figure 10.1).

Novice teacher. The *novice phase* begins when preservice teachers first encounter practicum experiences as part of their teacher education program and continues through student teaching and the intern experience.

Apprentice teacher. The *apprentice phase* begins for most teachers when they receive responsibility for planning and delivering instruction on their own. This phase continues until integration and synthesis of knowledge, pedagogy, and confidence emerges, marking the beginning of the professional period. Typically, the apprentice phase includes the induction period and extends into the second or third year of teaching.

Professional teacher. The *professional phase* emerges as teachers grow in their self-confidence as educators. Student feedback plays a critical role in this process. Students' respect for teachers and teachers' respect for students form the bedrock foundation upon which this stage is built.

Expert teacher. The *expert phase* symbolizes achievement of the high standards desired by the NCTAF (1996). Even if they do not formally seek it, these teachers meet the expectations required for national certification (Steffy, 1989). The goal of the model is to assure that all teachers develop their skills to operate at this expert level.

Distinguished teacher. The *distinguished phase* is reserved for teachers who are truly gifted in their field. They exceed current expectations for what teachers are expected to know and do. These teachers are the leaders of the profession. Distinguished teachers impact education-related decisions at city, state, and national levels.

Emeritus teacher. The *emeritus phase* begins with formal retirement. Teachers at this phase are those who want to continue to make a contribution to the field.

The six phases of the model are shown in Figure 10.1. The novice phase is the ideal time to learn skills in how to reflect. If a teacher's preservice training did not include opportunities to learn these skills, it is all the more important that principals working with apprentice teachers

Figure 10.1 The Life Cycle Model of the Classroom Teacher

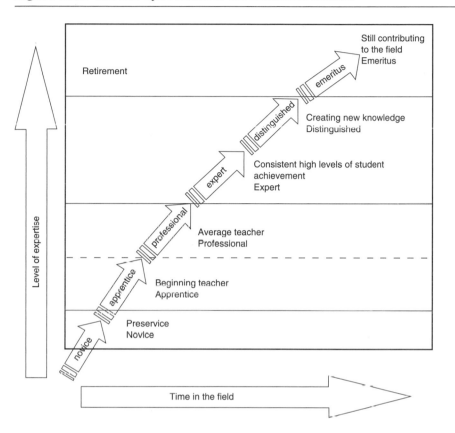

provide this training. A typical district may have anywhere from 10 to 20 percent of its teachers in the apprentice phase, depending on how many new hires the district is experiencing each year. Teachers at this level need more frequent walk-throughs and dependent-direct feedback.

The largest percentage of teachers currently working in schools is at the professional level. These teachers vary in the type of reflective inquiry they want or need.

The expert phase represents those teachers who are highly skilled. Students in these teachers' classes consistently achieve at high levels no matter what accountability test is in use. Unfortunately, it is typical for principals not to make frequent visits to these expert teachers' classrooms. This is a mistake. Expert teachers want their principals to make frequent classroom visits. They enjoy thinking and dialoguing about practice and flourish from engaging in interdependent, reflective conversations with the principal. While the number of teachers at this phase varies from district to district, they typically account for about 15 to 20 percent.

Teachers at the distinguished phase are those who are recognized for making contributions at the state and national level. These teachers are usually few in number.

As depicted in Figure 10.2, the boxes moving up and across the page are meant to show growth over time. As teachers move from apprentice to professional to expert, their skills and expertise are expanding. The basic premise of the model is that this growth occurs through a process of reflection, growth, and renewal. Through reflection, teachers think about their practice and seek ways to improve; this expands their skills and they feel a sense of renewal. It is a self-perpetuating cycle. The more they reflect, the more they grow.

Included in this model is the concept of withdrawal. This can be characterized as a loss of engagement, a moving away from taking responsibility for student learning. There is recognition that there are always forces within the social context of schools that have a negative impact on personnel. The goal is to minimize these forces. For some teachers, the lack of communication with the building principal can lead to disengagement

Figure 10.2 Career Tension in the Life Cycle Model

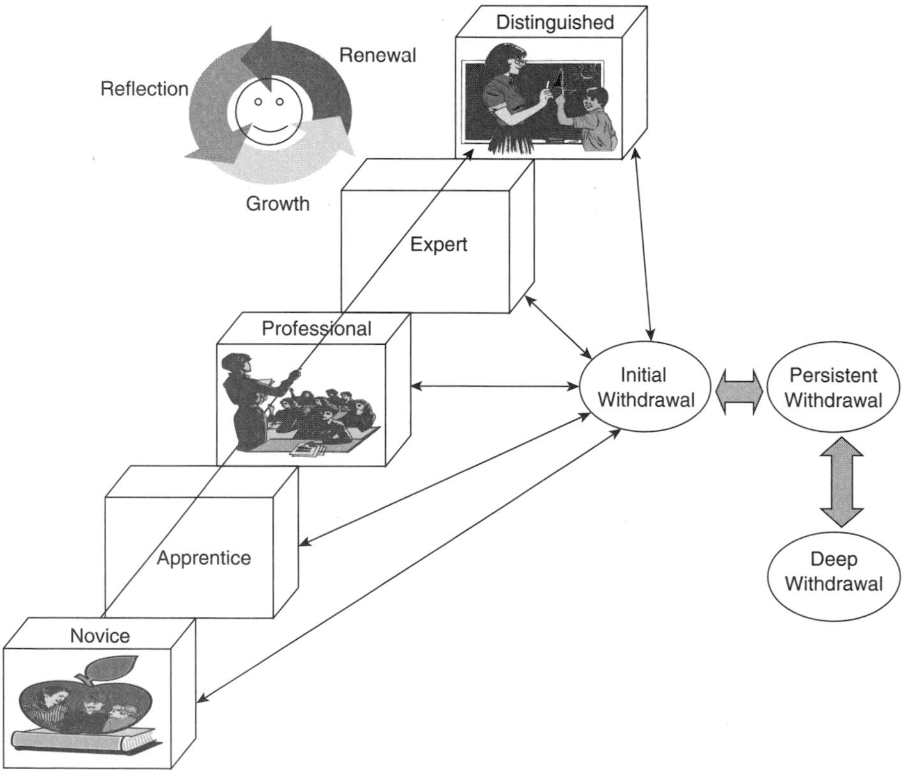

or withdrawal. It is not unusual for teachers to comment that they feel the building principal doesn't know or care about what they are doing in their classrooms. Implementation of the walk-through process would prevent this source of withdrawal.

The concept of reflection is not only fundamental to the life cycle model, it is fundamental to the walk-through process and transformative learning.

TRANSFORMATIVE LEARNING AS IT RELATES TO THE MODEL

As developed by Jack Mezirow (1991), transformative learning is "not so much what happens to people but how they interpret and explain what happens to them that determines their actions, their hopes, their contentment and emotional well-being, and their performance." The beginning of the idea of transformative learning can be traced to the publication in 1978 of a grounded theory field study about women returning to community college (Mezirow, 1978). The concept of *perspective transformation* emerged from that study. Perspective transformation referred to becoming aware of one's context, that is, the biographical, historical, and cultural underpinning of one's beliefs. Through this self-knowledge, assumptions and expectations are restructured. "This change constituted a learned transformation: the process resulting from it was designated transformative learning" (Mezirow, 1991). Mezirow sees adulthood as a transformative process that includes alienation from roles, developing new ways of knowing, and regenerating life with greater vigor.

The life cycle model can be considered an application of Mezirow's transformative theory. As teachers progress through their careers, they can engage in transformational processes such as critical reflection on practice and a redefinition of assumptions and beliefs that lead to enhanced self-worth. Or they can disengage from the work environment as a source and stimulation for new learning and begin the gradual decline into professional withdrawal. We posit that one of the essential roles of principals is to promote transformative learning among all staff, but especially among teachers.

ORGANIZATIONAL LEARNING AND TRANSFORMATION

There is a growing body of literature dealing with learning organizations (Senge, 1990; Watkins & Marsick, 1993; West, 1996; Yorks, O'Neil, &

Marsick, 1999). Karl Weick (1969) is given credit for first articulating the idea of the learning organization. However, the concept is rooted in the group dynamics literature going back to Lewin's (1958) seminal work. Organizational learning and transformation recognizes that the results of group learning often transcend the learning of individuals within the group (Yorks & Marsick, 2000). Organizational learning is designed to transform the organization, not just the individuals in the organization (West, 1996). Yorks and Marsick (2000) posit that two strategies account for transformative learning for individuals, groups, and/or organizations: action learning and collaborative inquiry. "Both action learning (AL) and collaborative inquiry (CI) are highly participatory and designed to foster learning from experience through cycles of action and subsequent reflection on that action" (p. 255).

Yorks et al. (1999) set forth a model depicting how reflection can result from problem-solving situations. The most elementary level of the model is called *incidental reflection*. At this level, there is discussion around an issue directed toward problem solving and implementation of solutions. *Content reflection* includes problem solving and reframing. At this level, participants learn a "process for learning."

At the content and process reflection level, participants begin to relate problem solving to personal goals and learning styles. The final level is called the *critical reflection* school and includes content, process, and premise reflection (Yorks & Marsick, 2000). Reflection is the most critical component of this level. It is here that participants challenge their basic beliefs.

We believe that as teachers move from one phase of the life cycle model to another, there is an accumulation of many critical reflection experiences that change the basic beliefs of teachers to the point where they are propelled into the next phase of the model. Critical reflection is the engine that propels them forward. Yorks and Marsick (2000) call collaborative inquiry a cousin to action learning: "Collaborative inquiry is a process consisting of repeated episodes of reflection and action through which a group of peers strives to answer a question of importance to them" (p. 266). This process simultaneously emphasizes participation, holistic understanding of experience, and democracy, and is viewed by Yorks and Marsick as more likely to lead to transformative learning. There are key differences in the two approaches. CI is a voluntary process in which participants seek out others to dialogue with who share their interests. The group defines how they will go about this process of inquiry and decides the formulation of the specific question to be studied by the group. When walk-through observations lead to group discussion and reflection, transformative learning takes place.

When individual critical reflection is combined with group problem solving and critical reflection, the likelihood for more rapid transformation is enhanced. Central office administrators and principals can be instrumental in creating an adult learning environment that supports this transformation from novice to expert teacher. At the same time, it is understood that all participants in this process are not equally ready to confront their basic attitudes and beliefs. As Yorks and Marsick (2000) state, "It depends in large part on the readiness of the learner to confront, rather than resist, the experience."

We would argue that the readiness level of the apprentice teacher is higher than that of the teacher who has developed a patterned response to problems and rarely questions his or her fundamental beliefs. By providing the apprentice teacher with a learning environment in which there is an expectation that critical reflection is the norm and that all teachers are expected to reach the expert level, we believe that over time the number of expert teachers will dramatically increase. The professional phase will be seen as a place where potential expert teachers are improving their skills as they move toward their ultimate goal.

While the application of transformative learning theory to organizational settings is in its infancy, it does hold promise for informing how we construct a learning environment to support the life cycle model for both teachers and principals. Guidelines for what this environment would look like might be drawn from Yorks and Marsick's (2000) integration of transformative learning theory and critical theory.

- Learners develop a critical engagement with their organizational and social world, increasingly recognizing that the existing state of affairs does not exhaust all possibilities and arriving at alternative courses of action.
- Learners develop an increasingly critical account of the cultural conditions on which their own habits of mind are based.
- Learners develop a commitment to a continuing critical examination of their points of view and habits of mind.
- Critical examination makes them more aware of how their historicity has influenced their existing habits of mind.
- Learners are confronted with alternative interpretations of their experiences in ways that make visible both their strengths and weaknesses, as well as the reasons behind their blind spots and misunderstandings. Capacity is enhanced for incorporating their insights into more inclusive and permeable habits of mind. (p. 276)

PROVIDING FEEDBACK
CONVERSATION FOR GROWTH

Teaching is a complicated, complex act. It demands the capability of integrating myriad interdependent acts within a social context that is very fluid. This social context is continuously shaped, modified, and changed by the characteristics of the students being taught, the nature of the content, and the environment in which the instruction is taking place. Within this dynamic mix, there is no all-inclusive way to shape effective teaching. Over the course of a professional lifetime, teachers grow in their ability to create, manage, and shape this learning culture. For many years, the role of reflection has been one concept that has been thought to connect to improved teacher competence over time, and it is also generally accepted that there is a link between teacher reflection and improved student learning.

Reflection is an important human activity in which people recapture their experience, think about it, mull it over, and evaluate it. It is this working with experience that is important in learning. The capacity to reflect is developed to different stages in different people, and it may be this ability that characterized those who learn effectively from experience (Boud, Keogh, & Walker, 1985).

Teachers who have this capacity to reflect on practice tend to possess what Dewey (1933) described as the attitudes necessary for engaging in reflection. They are open-mindedness, wholeheartedness, and responsibility. We take the position that these are attitudes typical of the apprentice teacher and that they can be cultivated in teachers and promoted in them by the building principal. In fact, by using the walk-through process, the expectation is that the willingness to reflect will become the norm for the building. Among the three phases of apprentice, professional, and expert, the willingness to reflect is strongest at the apprentice level. Without the engagement of the principal, apprentice teachers tend to get caught up in the routines of lesson planning and delivery and spend less time in reflection. If the principal sets the tone that the culture of the learning environment thrives on active reflection among all of the teaching staff, then the process becomes integrated into the daily routine of teaching. Without this focus, teacher reflection tends to be an idiosyncratic practice of just a few individuals rather than a defining characteristic of the learning environment. By engaging in reflective feedback in the walk-through process, principals help teachers internalize and value the reflective act.

Becoming a reflective practitioner is a skill that can be taught. It begins by creating a learning environment where the characteristics of open-mindedness, wholeheartedness, and responsibility are cultivated.

The principal is key to setting an open-minded tone for this learning environment. The learning environment must be one where many different ideas and suggestions are welcomed, discussed, and explored. Professionals in this learning environment are active listeners. They are willing to hear from others who may have ideas that are not part of a shared belief system. People working in this type of school are open to questioning past practices that may not have led to achieving desired results.

Wholeheartedness is exemplified in this learning environment by people actively engaged in pursuing methods and mechanisms to improve practice. In this environment there is no tacit, superficial engagement or acceptance of ideas in theory, nor does practice remain typified by ineffective strategies. Rather, there is a feeling of gusto, commitment, and thirst for creative new ideas and challenging thinking. In fact, creativity is acknowledged as a mark of leadership (see Simonton, 1994). There is an overall desire for knowledge that is promoted by the principal and staff. This type of learning environment is not reserved just for faculty. It permeates the classroom as well and promotes the same attitudes among students.

A learning environment labeled as responsible is one where everyone is willing to be held accountable for achieving results. This is not an environment where teachers routinely blame parents and students for lack of student success. Accepting responsibility is closely connected to being willing to accept the consequences of one's actions. For open-mindedness, wholeheartedness, and responsibility to be the accepted attitudes for people within the organization, these characteristics must also be modeled and encouraged by the building principal and then the two, attitude and environment, go hand in hand. In reality they can be created jointly, with the walk-through process serving as a catalyst for this endeavor.

References

Andrews, R., & Soder, R. (1987). Principal leadership and student achievement. *Educational Leadership, 44*(6), 9–11.

Andrews, R., Soder, R., & Jacoby, D. (1986, April). *Principal roles, other in-school variables, and academic achievement by ethnicity and SES.* Paper presented at the annual meeting of the American Educational Research Association, San Francisco. (ERIC Document Reproduction Service No. ED 268 664)

Anglin, L., Goldman, R., & Anglin, J. (1982). *Teaching: What's it all about.* NewYork: Harper & Row.

Annunziata, J. (1997). Linking teacher evaluation and professional development. In J. Stronge (Ed.), *Evaluating teaching: A guide to current thinking and best practice* (pp. 288–301). Thousand Oaks, CA: Corwin Press.

Ashton, P., & Webb, R. (1986). *Making a difference: Teachers' sense of efficacy and student achievement.* New York: Longman.

Baltes, P., & Schaie, K. (1976). On the plasticity of intelligence in adulthood and old age: Where Horn and Donaldson fail. *American Psychologist, 31,* 720–725.

Bell, B., & Gilbert, J. (1996). *Teacher development.* Washington, DC: Falmer.

Bell, C. (1998). *Managers as mentors: Building partnerships for learning.* San Francisco: Berrett-Koehler.

Berne, E. (1963). *The structure and dynamics of organizations and groups.* New York: Grove.

Blair, J. (2000). Teacher idealism tempered by frustration, survey finds. *Education Week, 19*(38), 6.

Blase, J. (1987). Dimensions of effective school leadership: The teacher's perspective. *American Educational Research Journal, 24,* 589–610.

Blase, J., & Blase, J. (1998). *Handbook of instructional leadership.* Thousand Oaks, CA: Corwin Press.

Bloom, B., Engelhard, M., Furst, E., Hill, W., & Krathwohl, D. (1956). *Taxonomy of educational objectives: Cognitive domain.* White Plains, NY: David McKay.

Blount, J. (1999). Manliness and the gendered construction of school administration in the USA. *International Journal of Leadership in Education: Theory and Practice, 2,* 55–68.

Boud, D., Keogh, R., & Walker, D. (1985). *Reflection: Turning experience into learning.* London: Kogan Page.

Calabrese, R. (2002). *The leadership assignment: Creating change.* Boston: Allyn & Bacon.

Carr, M. (2002). The principal: An authority, an educator, an advocate. *Newsleader, 49*(7), 3.

Cate, J. M. (2002). Walk through supervision can help improve social studies instruction. *National Social Studies Supervisors' Association Newsletter, 15*(3), 5–7.

Cezak, G., Webb, L., & Kalohn, J. (1995). The use of cognitive taxonomies in licensure and certification test development: Reasonable or customary? *Evaluation and the Health Professions, 18*(1), 77–91.

Chester, M., & Beaudin, B. (1996). Efficacy beliefs of newly hired teachers in urban schools. *American Educational Research Journal, 33*, 233–257.

Cogan, M. (1973). *Clinical supervision.* Boston: Houghton Mifflin.

Costa, A. L. (1994). *Cognitive coaching: A foundation for renaissance schools.* Norwood, MA: Christopher-Gordon.

Costa, A. L., & Garmston, R. (1985, February). Supervision for intelligent teaching. *Educational Leadership, 42*(5), 70–80.

Covey, S. R. (1989). *The seven habits of highly effective people.* New York: Simon & Schuster.

Csikszentmihalyi, M. (1990). *Flow: The psychology of optimal experience.* New York: Harper & Row.

Culbertson, J. (1996). *Building bridges: The mission and principles of professional development.* Washington, DC: U. S. Department of Education, Government Printing Office. (ERIC Document Reproduction Service No. ED 404 322)

Darling-Hammond, L. (1990). Achieving our goals: Superficial or structural reforms? *Phi Delta Kappan, 72*(4), 286–295.

Darling-Hammond, L., & McLaughlin, M. (1995). Policies that support professional development in an era of reform. *Phi Delta Kappan, 76*, 597–604.

Deutsch, M. (1949). A theory of co-operation and competition. *Human Relations, 2*, 129–152.

Dewey, J. (1944). *Democracy and education.* New York: MacMillan. (Original work published 1916) Electronic version: http://www.ilt.columbia.edu/publications/dewey.html

Dewey, J. (1933). *How we think.* New York: Heath.

Dewey, J. (1974). *John Dewey on education: Selected writings.* Chicago: University of Chicago Press.

Dilts, R., Allborn, T., & Smith, S. (1990). *Beliefs: Pathways to health and well-being.* Portland, OR: Metamorphous.

Downey, C. J. (2002). *Questioning strategies* [Online module]. Houston, TX: Houston Independent School District.

Downey C. J., & Frase L. E. (2001). *Participant's manual for conducting walk-through with reflective feedback to maximize student achievement* (2nd ed.). Huxley, IA: Curriculum Management Services.

Duke, D. (1995). Speculations on the future of teacher evaluation and educational accountability. In D. Duke (Ed.), *Teacher evaluation policy: From accountability to professional development* (pp. 189–197). Albany: State University of New York Press.

Educational Research Service. (1998). *ERS informed educator: Ability grouping: effects and alternatives.* Washington, DC: Educational Research Service.

Eisner, E. (2002). The kind of schools we need. *Phi Delta Kappan, 83*, 576–583.

Ellis, A., & Fouts, J. (1993). *Research on educational innovations.* Princeton Junction, NJ: Eye on Education.

Elmore, R. (2000). *Building a new structure for school leadership.* Washington, DC: Albert Shanker Institute.

English, F. (1988). *Curriculum auditing.* Lancaster, PA: Technomic.

English, F. (2001). [Unpublished notes at from a walk-through training, San Diego, CA.]

English, F. (1993). *Deciding what to teach and test.* Newbury Park, CA: Corwin Press.

English, F., & Steffy, B. (2001). *Deep curriculum alignment: Creating a level playing field for all children on high-stakes tests of educational accountability.* Lanham, MD: Scarecrow.

English, F. W. (1988, Summer). *Curriculum management audit training.* Montreal, Quebec, Canada: American Association of School Administrators.

Erikson, E. (1968). *Identity, youth and crisis.* New York: Norton.

Fairclough, N. (1992). *Discourse and social change.* Cambridge, UK: Polity.

Farkas, S., Johnson, J., & Foleno, T. (2000). *A sense of calling: Who teaches and why.* New York: Public Agenda Foundation. (ERIC Document Reproduction Service No. ED 443 815)

Fessler, R., & Christensen, J. (1992). *The teacher career cycle: Understanding and guiding the professional development of teachers.* Boston: Allyn & Bacon.

Foucault, M. (1972). *The archaeology of knowledge and the discourse of language.* New York: Pantheon.

Frase, L. (1998a). *An examination of the relationships among principal classroom visits, teacher flow experiences, efficacy, and student cognitive engagement in two inner city school districts.* Paper presented at the 1998 annual meeting of the American Educational Research Association, Seattle, WA.

Frase, L. (1998b, April). *An examination of teachers' flow experiences, efficacy, and instructional leadership in large inner-city and urban school districts.* Paper presented at the annual meeting of the American Educational Research Association, San Diego, CA. (ERIC Document Reproduction Service No. ED 421 599)

Frase, L. (2001, April 10–14). *A confirming study of the predictive power of principal classroom visits on efficacy and teacher flow experiences.* Paper presented at the annual meeting of the American Educational Research Association, Seattle, WA.

Frase, L. (2003). *Policy implications for school work environments: Implications from a causal model regarding frequency of teacher flow experiences, school principal classroom walk-throughs, teacher evaluation and professional development, and efficacy measures.* Paper presented at the Annual Meeting of the American Education Research Association, Chicago.

Frase, L. (in press). New wine and new bottles: Pedagogical fundamentals and theory. In F. W. English (Ed.), *Handbook of educational leadership: New dimensions and realities.* Thousand Oaks, CA: Sage.

Frase, L., Downey, C., & Canciamilla, L. (1999). Putting principals in their place: The classroom. *Thrust for Educational Leadership, 28*(5), 36–39.

Frase, L., & Hetzel, R. (1990). *School management by wandering around.* Lancaster, PA: Technomic.

Frase, L., & Streshly, W. (1994). Lack of accuracy, feedback, and commitment in teacher evaluation. *Journal of Personnel Evaluation in Education, 8*(1), 47–57.

Frase, L., & Streshly, W. (2000). *The top ten myths in education: Fantasies Americans love to believe.* Landham, MD: Scarecrow.

Freedman, B. (2003, January). *Principal visibility and classroom walk-throughs: Supporting instructional leadership and school improvement.* Paper presented at the International Congress of School Effectiveness and School Improvement Annual Conference, Sydney, Australia.

Freedman, B., & LaFleur, C. (2002, April). *Making leadership visible and practical: Walking for improvement.* Paper delivered at the American Educational Research Association Convention, New Orleans, LA.

Freedman, B., & LaFleur, C. (2003, January). *Principal visibility and classroom walk-throughs: Supporting instructional leadership and school improvement.* Paper presented at the International Congress of School Effectiveness and School Improvement, Sydney, Australia.

Fullan, M. (1995). The limits and the potential of professional development. In T. Guskey & M. Huberman (Eds.), *Professional development in education: New paradigms and practices* (pp. 253–267). New York: Teachers College Press.

Fullan, M. (2001). *Leading in a culture of change.* San Francisco: Jossey-Bass.

Furth, H. (1981). *Piaget and knowledge.* Chicago: University of Chicago Press.

Galloway, F., & Frase, L. (2003). *A methodological primer for estimating the effects of flow in the classroom.* Paper presented at the Annual Meeting of the American Education Research Association, Chicago.

Glasser, W. (1992). *The quality school.* New York: Harper & Row.

Glickman, C. (1991). Pretending not to know what we know. *Educational Leadership, 48,* 4–10.

Glickman, D., Gordon, S., & Ross-Gordon, J. (1995). *Supervision of instruction: A developmental approach.* Boston: Allyn & Bacon.

Glickman, D., Gordon, S., & Ross-Gordon, J., (1998). *Supervision of instruction: A developmental approach* (4th ed.). Needham Heights, MA: Allyn & Bacon.

Goddard, R., Hoy, W., & Hoy, A. (2000). Collective teacher efficacy: Its meaning, measure, and impact on student achievement. *American Educational Research Journal, 37,* 479–507.

Good, T., & Brophy, J. (2000). *Looking in classrooms* (8th ed.). New York: Addison-Wesley.

Goodlad, J., & Anderson, R. (1963). *The non-graded elementary school.* New York: Harcourt, Brace & World.

Gould, S. J. (2002). *The structure of evolutionary theory.* Cambridge, MA: Belknap Press of Harvard University Press.

Gray, P., & Frase, L. (2003, July 20). *Analysis of teacher flow experiences as they relate to principal classroom walk-throughs.* [Unpublished data from report to Shawnee Mission School Board, Shawnee Mission, KS.]

Greenleaf, R. (Spears, L., Ed.). (1996). *The power of servant leadership.* San Francisco: Berrett-Koehler.

Haefele, D. (1993). Evaluating teachers: A call for change. *Journal of Personnel Evaluation in Education, 7*(1), 21–31.

Hall, G., & Hord, S. (2000). *Implementing change: Patterns, principles, and potholes.* Boston: Allyn & Bacon.

Hallinger, P., & Heck, R. (1996). Reassessing the principal's role in school effectiveness: A review of empirical research, 1980–1995. *Educational Administration Quarterly, 32,* 5–44.

Heck, R. (1991). *The effects of school context and principal leadership on school climate and school achievement.* Paper presented at the annual meeting of the American Educational Research Association, San Francisco.

Heck, R. (1992). Principals' instructional leadership and school performance: Implications for policy development. *Educational Evaluation and Policy Analysis, 14,* 21–34.

Heck, R., Larsen, T., & Marcoulides, G. (1990). Instructional leadership and school achievement: Validation of a causal model. *Educational Administration Quarterly, 26,* 94–125.

Heist, P., & Yonge, G. (1968). *Omnibus Personality Inventory.* University of California, Berkeley, Center for Studies in Education.

Huberman, M. (1993). *The lives of teachers.* New York: Teachers College Press.

Hunt, D. (1971). *Matching models of education.* Toronto, Ontario, Canada: Institute for Studies in Education.

Hunter, M. (1968). [Unpublished notes taken by C. Downcy at training conducted in Arizona by the Arizona School Administrator's Association.]

Katz, D., & Kahn, R. L. (1966). *The social psychology of organizations.* New York: John Wiley.

Kohlberg, L. (1969). Stage and sequence: The cognitive-developmental approach to socialization. In D. Goslin (Ed.), *The handbook of socialization theory and research* (pp. 349–480). New York: Rand McNally.

Lambert, L., Walker, D., Zimmerman, D., Cooper, J., Lambert, M., Gardner, M., & Slack, P. (1995). *The constructivist leader.* New York: Teachers College Press.

Lawler, E. (1971). *Pay and organizational effectiveness: A psychological view.* New York: McGraw-Hill.

Levinson, D., Darrow, C., Klein, E., Levinson, M., & McKee, B. (1978). *The seasons of a man's life.* New York: Knopf.

Lewin, K. (1958). Group decision and social change. In G. E. Swanson, T. M. Newcomb, & E. L. Hartley (Eds.), *Readings in social psychology* (Rev. ed., pp. 459–473). New York: Henry Holt.

Loevinger, J. (1976). *Ego development.* San Francisco: Jossey-Bass.

Loevinger, J. (1987). *Paradigms of personality.* New York: Freeman.

Marczely, B. (2001). *Supervision in education: A differentiated approach with legal perspectives.* Gaithersburg, MD: Aspen.

Marzano, R. (2001). *A handbook for classroom instruction that works.* Alexandria, VA: Association for Supervision and Curriculum Development.

Marzano, R., Pickering, D., & Pollock, J. (2001). *Classroom instruction that works: Research-based strategies for increasing student achievement.* Alexandria, VA: Association for Supervision and Curriculum Development.

McGregor, D. (1966). *Leadership and motivation: Essays of Douglas McGregor.* Cambridge: MIT Press.

McKenna, J. (1993). Close encounters of the executive kind: Regrettably, for boss and subordinates alike, they're few in number. *Industry Week, 242*(17), 13–18.

Medley, D., Coker, H., & Soar, R. (1984). *Measurement-based evaluation of teacher performance: An empirical approach.* New York: Longman.

Mezirow, J. (1978). *Education for perspective transformation: Women's re-entry programs in community colleges.* New York: Teachers College Press, Columbia University.

Mezirow, J. (1991). *Transformative dimensions of adult learning.* San Francisco: Jossey-Bass.

National Commission on Teaching and America's Future. (1996). *What matters most: Teaching for America's future.* New York: Author. (ERIC Document Reproduction Service No. ED 395 931)

Nevo, D. (1994). How can teachers benefit from teacher evaluation? *Journal of Personnel Evaluation in Education, 8*(2), 109–117.

Oliva, P., & Pawlas, G. (1997). *Supervision for today's schools.* New York: Longman.

Orlich, D., Remaley, A., & Facemyer, K. (1993). Seeking the link between student achievement and staff development. *Journal of Staff Development, 14*(3), 2–17.

Peters, T., & Waterman, R. Jr., (1984). *In search of excellence: Lessons from America's best-run companies.* New York: Warner.

Piaget, J. (1954). *The construction of reality in the child* (M. Cook, Trans.). New York: Basic Books.

Pines, A., Aronson, E., & Kafrey, D. (1981). *Burnout: From tedium to personal growth.* New York: Free Press.

Public Agenda Foundation. (1995). *Professional development for teachers: The public's view.* New York: Author.

Reiman, A., & Thies-Sprinthall, L. (1998). *Mentoring and supervision for teacher development.* New York: Longman.

Sagor, R. (1992). Three principals who make a difference. *Educational Leadership, 49*(5), 13–18.

Scholastic, Inc. (2000). *Scholastic/CCSSO teacher voices 2000 survey.* Washington, DC: Author.

Scriven, M. (1967). The methodology of evaluation. In R. Stake (Ed.), *Perspectives on curriculum evaluation.* Chicago: Rand McNally.

Scriven, M. (1981). Summative teacher evaluation. In J. Millman (Ed.), *Handbook of teacher evaluation* (pp. 244–271). Beverly Hills, CA: Sage.

Scriven, M. (1988). *Evaluating teachers as professionals.* Nedlands: University of Western Australia. (ERIC Document Reproduction Service No. ED 300 882)

Senge, P. (1990). *The fifth discipline: The art and practice of the learning organization.* New York: Doubleday.

Sergiovanni, T. (1999). *The lifeworld of leadership: Creating culture, community, and personal meaning in our schools.* San Francisco: Jossey-Bass.

Shakeshaft, C. (1989). *Women in educational administration.* Newbury Park, CA: Corwin Press.

Simonton, D. (1994). *Greatness.* New York: Guilford.

Slavin, R. (1989). PET and the pendulum: Faddism in education and how to stop it. *Phi Delta Kappan, 70,* 752–758.

Smith, J., & Blase, J. (1991). From empiricism to hermeneutics: Educational leadership as a practical and moral activity. *Journal of Educational Administration, 29*(1), 6–21.

Snarey, J. (1985). Cross-cultural universality of socio-moral development. *Psychological Bulletin, 97*(2), 202–232.

Soar, R., Medley, D., & Coker, H. (1983). Teacher evaluation: A critique of currently used methods. *Phi Delta Kappan, 65,* 239–246.

Steffy, B. (1989). *Career stages of classroom teachers.* Lancaster, PA: Technomic.

Steffy, B., & Wolfe, M. (1997). *The life cycle of the career teacher: Maintaining excellence for a lifetime.* West Lafayette, IN: Kappa Delta Pi International.

Steffy, B., Wolfe, M., Pasch, S., & Enz, B. (Eds.). (2000). *The life cycle of the career teacher.* Thousand Oaks, CA: Corwin Press.

Tanner, D., & Tanner, L. (1987). *Supervision in education: Problems and practices.* New York: Macmillan.

Teddlie, C., Kirby, P., & Stringfield, S. (1989). Effective versus ineffective schools: Observable differences in the classroom. *American Journal of Education, 97,* 221–236.

Thorndike, R. (1913). The psychology of learning. *Educational Psychology, 2.*

Thorndike, R. (1951). Community variables as predictors of intelligence and academic achievement. *Journal of Educational Psychology, 42,* 321–338.

Tileston, D. (2000). *Ten best teaching practices: How brain research, learning styles, and standards define teaching competencies.* Thousand Oaks, CA: Corwin Press.

Trueman, W. (1991). CEO isolation and how to fight it. *Canadian Business, 64*(7), 28–32.

Valentine, J. W., Clark, D. C., Nickerson, N. C., & Keefe, J. W. (1981). *The middle school principal.* Reston, VA: National Association of Secondary School Principals.

Vgotsky, L. (1962). *Thought and language.* Cambridge: MIT Press.

Wagner, T. (2001, January). Leadership for learning: An action theory of school change. [Electronic version.] *Phi Delta Kappan.*

Watkins, K., & Marsick, V. (1993). *Sculpting the learning organization: Lessons in the art and science of systemic change.* San Francisco: Jossey-Bass.

Weick, K. (1969). *The social psychology of oganizing.* Reading, MA: Addison-Wesley.

Wells, H. G. (1961). *The outline of history: Being a plain history of life and mankind.* Garden City, NY: Garden City Books.

Welsh, S. W. (1971). [Unpublished notes taken by C. Downey at a training conducted in Arizona by Ms.Welch.]

West, G. (1996). Group learning in the workplace. In S. Imel (Ed.), *Learning in groups: Exploring fundamental principles, new uses, and emerging opportunities.* San Francisco: Jossey-Bass.

Whalen, S. P. (1997, March). *Assessing flow experiences in highly able adolescent learners.* Paper presented at the annual meeting of the American Educational Research Association, Chicago. (ERIC Document Reproduction Service No. ED 409 382)

Wimpleberg, R., Teddlie, C., & Stringfield, S. (1989). Sensitivity to context: The past and future of effective schools research. *Educational Administration Quarterly, 25,* 82–107.

Yorks, L., & Marsick, V. (2000). Organizational learning and transformation. In J. Mezirow & Associates, *Learning as transformation: Critical perspectives on theory in progress.* San Francisco: Jossey-Bass.

Yorks, L., O'Neil, J., & Marsick, V. (1999). Action learning: Theoretical bases and varieties of practice. In L.Yorks, J. O'Neil, & V. Marsick (Eds.), *Action learning: Effective strategies for individual, team, and organization development, Vol. 1(2): Academy of human resource development monograph series: Advances in developing human resources.* San Francisco: Berrett-Koehler.

Zhu, N. (2001). *The effects of teacher flow experience on the cognitive engagement of students.* Unpublished doctoral dissertation, University of San Diego.

Index

administrators. *See* principals; supervisors
adult-to-adolescent model of discourse, 11–12
adult-to-adult model of discourse, x, 11, 12, 60, 135
adult-to-child model of discourse, 11, 45
Allen, Woody, 157
Anderson, R., 141
Andrews, R., 149, 154, 156
Annunziata, J., 151, 152
Anton, Roger, 116
Aronson, E., 177
Ashton, P., 151
attributes, reflective questions and missing, 65–67

Baltes, P., 134
Beaudin, B., 149, 151
Bell, B., 177
Bell, Chip, 133
Berne, Eric, 11
Blair, J., 150
*Blase, J, 149, 154
Blase, Jo, 22, 46
Blase, Joseph, 22, 46
Bloom, B., 27, 28
board policies, and support for classroom walk-throughs, 107–8
Boud, D., 184
bureaucratic practices, and professional relationships, xi, 160–62, 170

career cycle of teachers, 177–81
Cate, J. M., 117
Cezak, G., 28
Chester, M., 149, 151
Christensen, J., 138

classroom practices. *See also* Management by Wandering Around (MBWA); teachers
and framing reflective questions, 87–90
and instructional decision points, 21, 33–34
mapping the dimensions of complexity in elementary school classrooms, 89
and MBWA, 149, 154
and reflective questions, 65, 72–73, 83–84
and relationships with teachers, xi
and teaching effectiveness, ix
and "walk the walls," 21, 35–36
classroom walk-throughs. *See also* Downey walk-through model
and comparison of approaches, 4
as discursive practice, 159–74
examining dimensions of, 163–64
examples of successful implementation, 116–23
Columbia-Brazoria Independent School District, 120–21
Durham and Simcoe Conty School Boards, 118–19
Napa Valley Schools, 119
Norman Public Schools, 117
Salinas Union High School District, 116–17
San Benito County, 122–23
San Leandro Unified School District, 121–22
Shawnee Mission School District, 119–200
find time for, 99–101
goals of, 8, 14

innovations and faddism, 141–58
background of MBWA, 143–45
research and theory base, 145–48
preparations for, 101–5
and parents, 101, 104–5
and students, 101–2, 104
and teachers, 101, 102–4
reasons for brief, 6
reflective questions about, 1–2, 17–18
and short classroom visits, xi, 125
value of, 5–9
clinical supervisory model, 132
coaches. *See* supervisors
Cogan, Morris, 132
Cognitive Coaching, 10
cognitive development theory, 134–37
Coker, H., 152
collaborative interaction model of
discourse, 60
collaborative-interdependent reflective
conversation, 76–78
collaborative reflective learning
environments, 139–40
comfort zone, of teachers, 22, 84–87
conversational sequences. *See also*
feedback conversations; follow-up
conversations
and collaborative-interdependent
reflective conversation, 76–77
and direct-dependent feedback,
52–56
Downey Reflective Conversation, 43
and indirect-independent reflection,
58–60
and interdependent-direct approach,
75–80
motivational approach, and
professional, 43
and reflective inquiry, 75–80
Cooper, J., 80
Costa, A. L., 10, 57
Covey, Stephen, 11
Csikszentmihalyi, M., 149
Culbertson, J., 151
curriculum content
and deep alignment, 27
and Downey walk-through, 3
and five-step observation informal
walk-throughs, 21, 23–33

and reflective questions, 65, 72–73
and teaching effectiveness, ix
and topological alignment, 27
troubleshooting Downey walk-through
model, and lack of adequate
curriculum, 171–72
Curriculum Management Systems, Inc.
(CMSi), 108

Darling-Hammond, L., 152
Darrow, C., 177
dependent feedback statements. *See* direct
feedback statements
Deutsch, Morton, 153
developmental supervisory practices,
131–34
Dewey, John, 114, 137, 184
dialogues, 48
Dickson, Pat, 121–22
dimensions of classroom walk-throughs,
examining, 163–64
"dipstick" model of supervision, xi
direct feedback statements, 45–56
and conversational sequences, 52–56
direct-dependent feedback, 43
direct interaction model of discourse,
5, 45
and notes about observations, 46–48
and novice/apprentice teachers, 49
practice form for, 56
and 6th-grade mathematics scenario, 51
and 12th-grade language arts
scenario, 51
discourse theory, 174
discursive practices, 159–74
from corrective to discursive
supervision, 164–66
examining dimensions of classroom
walk-throughs, 163–64
principal-teacher interactions, model
of, ix, xi, 161–62
vs. bureaucratic practices, 160–62
vs. traditional supervisory practices,
160–61
discussions/dialogues, 48
Downey, Carolyn J.
and curriculum decision points, 26
and evolution of classroom
walk-through process, 9

and "feedback," 42
reasons for brief classroom
walk-throughs, 6
and reflective questions, 67
Downey Reflective Conversation,
9, 43, 58–60, 76–77
Downey Reflective Question, 43.
See also reflective inquiry
Downey walk-through model,
See also classroom walk-throughs
change, and process vs. outcome,
167–70
description of, 2–5, 8
evolution of, 9–15
and normative gaze, 166–67
stages in implementation process of, 168
technical approach, and assumptions
about, 166
troubleshooting problems, 171–74
Duke, D., 152

educational cultures
changes in, ix, xi, 109–24
challenges and barriers to, 112–14
history of, 110–12
and marginal teachers, 114–16
principals and changes in, 112
student(s) and challenges and
barriers to change in, 113–14
and reflective inquiry, 125–40
and cognitive development theory,
134–37
and developmental supervisory
practices, 131–34
history of, 126–31
and teachers, promoting
development of, 137–40
Educational Research Service, 113
efficiency issues, and supervision of
teachers, x
egalitarian model of professional
practice, x
Eisner, Elliot, 144
elementary school classrooms
mapping the dimensions of
complexity in, 89
Ellis, A., 142, 145
Elmore, Richard, 7
Englehard, M., 28

English, Fenwick
and deep alignment of curriculum,
12, 23, 26, 27, 31
and educational cultures, results of
changes in, 124
Enz., B., 176
Erikson, E., 177
evaluation issues, and supervision of
teachers, x, 10, 141–42, 173, 174

Facemyer, K., 152
Fairclough, N., 159, 174
Farkas, S., 150
feedback conversations. See also
conversational sequences
and direct, use of, 45–56
and direct statements, 48–56
and discussions/dialogues, 48
and growth of teachers, 184–85
and notes about observations, 43–45,
46–48
use of word "feedback," 43
Fessler, R., 138
five elements of reflective questions,
67–72, 73–75
five-step observation informal
walk-throughs, 18–20, 41
curricular decision points, 21, 23–33
flowchart for, 41
instructional decision points, 21,
33–34
safety and health issues, 21, 36
student orientation to work, 21–23
"walk the walls"–curricular and
instructional decision, 21,
35–36
worksheet for, 38–40
Florida practice tests, 29
Foleno, T., 150
follow-up conversations. See also
conversational sequences
comparison of approaches to, 14–15
and dialogue paradigm for classroom
walk-throughs, 43, 44–45
and Downey walk-through, 3
and reflective inquiry, 43, 52
by supervisors with teachers, 7–8
Foucault, Michael, 174
Fouts, J., 142, 145

framing reflective questions
and instructional practices, 87–90
Frase, Larry E.
and cultivating educational
cultures, 123
and curriculum decision points, 26
and "feedback," 42
and MBWA, 144, 149, 151, 152, 154
and professionalization of educational
culture, 130
reasons for brief classroom
walk-throughs, 6
and reflective questions, 67
and teacher attitudes toward teacher
appraisals, 153
Freedman, Beverly, 118, 123, 155
Freedman, Beverly, 149
Fullan, M., 151
Fullan, Michael, 110
Furst, E., 28
Furth, H., 137

Galloway, F., 149
Gardner, M., 80
gender discrimination, and supervisory
practices, ix, x
Gilbert, J., 177
Glasser, W., 48
Glickman, Carl, 9, 113, 132
Goddard, R., 153, 154
Goodlad, J., 141
Gordon, S., 132
"gotcha" model of supervision, x–xi, 87
Gould, Stephen J., 142
Gray, P., 155
Greenleaf, R., 116

Haefele, D., 152
Hall, Gene, 8
Hallinger, P., 156
Harrington, Bill, 120
Harrison, South Dakota, Board
of Education, 127–28
Heck, R., 149, 154, 156
Hetzel, R., 144
Hewlett-Packard (H-P), 144
Hill, W., 28
Hord, Shirley, 8
Hoy, A., 151

Hoy, W., 151
Huberman, M., 138
Hunt, D., 135
Hunter, Madeline, 10
Hunter model of teacher evaluation,
10, 141–42

independent-direct approach, 43
indirect-independent conversational
sequences, 58–60
indirect-independent reflection, 58–60
indirect reflective inquiry, 57–60
industrial models for interactions,
x, 11–12
informal and collaborative aspects of
classroom walk-throughs, 5–6
instructional practices. *See* classroom
practices
interdependent-direct approach,
43, 60–75, 75–80

Jacoby, D., 156
Johnson, J., 150

Kafrey, D., 177
Kahn, R. L., 153
Kalohn, J., 28
Katz, D., 153
Keefe, J. W., 149, 154
Keogh, R., 184
Kirby, P., 149, 154
Klein, E., 177
Kohlberg, L., 135, 136
Krathwohl, D., 28

LaFleur, Clay, 118, 123, 149, 155
Lambert, L., 80
Lambert, M., 80
language of discourse, ix
Larsen, T., 149, 154
Lawler, E., 145
learning environments, 139–40
Levinson, D., 177
Lewin, K., 153
life cycle of career teacher model,
177–81
The Life Cycle of the Career Teacher Model
(Steffy et al.), 176
Lincoln, Abraham, 143–44

Loevinger, J., 135, 136, 177
Louis XVI, 144

Management by Wandering Around
(MBWA), 143–45
background of, 143–45
research and theory base for, 145,
148–55
classroom instruction, improved,
149, 154
student discipline and student
acceptance of advice and
criticism, improved, 149, 154
teacher attitudes toward professional
development, improved, 149,
151–52
teacher attitudes toward teacher
appraisal, improved, 149,
152–53
teacher efficacy of other teachers,
increase in perceived, 149, 153
teacher-perceived effectiveness of
school, improved, 149, 154–55
teacher perception of principal
effectiveness, improved, 149, 154
teacher satisfaction enhanced,
149–51
teacher self-efficacy, improved,
149, 151
Marcoulides, G., 149, 154
Marczely, B., 175
Marie Antoinette, 144
Marsick, V., 181, 182, 183
Marzano, R., 154
McArdle-Kulas, Olive, 119
McKee, B., 177
McKenna, J., 144
McLaughlin, M., 152
Medley, D., 152
mentoring, and supervisory practices, 133
Mezirow, J., 181
missing attributes, and reflective
questions, 65–67
models. See specific models
motivational approach, 43

National Commission on Teaching and
America's Future (NCTAF), 178
Nevo, D., 152

Nickerson, N. C., 149, 154
No Child Left Behind legislation, 131
notes, about observations, 43–45, 46–48
novice/apprentice teachers. See also
teachers
comfort zone of, 85–86, 87
and direct feedback statements, 49
and framing reflective questions,
85–86, 87
and notes, 43–44, 46
and teacher career development, 178

observation, 2–3
Oliva, P., 127–28, 129
O'Neil, J., 181–82, 182
Orlich, D., 152

parents, role of, xi, 101, 104–5
Pasch, S., 176
Pawlas, G., 127–28, 129
Peters, T., 144
Phi Delta Kappa (PDK), 108
Piaget, J., 177
Pines, A., 177
Powell, Colin, 144
principals
bureaucratic practices, and relationship
of teachers with, xi, 160–62, 170
and discursive practices, ix, xi, 161–62
and educational cultures, changes
in, 112
and normative gaze on teachers,
166–67
principal-teacher interactions, model
of, ix, xi
and relationship to teachers, ix, xi,
161–62, 166–70
and supervisory practices, ix–x, xi
and value of classroom walk-throughs,
7–8
and view of change as process vs.
outcome, 167–70
professionalization of supervisory
practices, 126–31
Public Agenda Foundation, 151
Pugh, Cole, 120

The Quality School (Glasser), 48
quetions. See reflective inquiry

record keeping, for classroom
walk-throughs, 105–7
reflective conversations, 9, 43, 58–60,
76–77
reflective inquiry
and attributes, missing, 65–67
and classroom practices, 83–84
comfort zone of, 84–85
and conversations, 75–80
and curriculum content, 65, 72–73
and defensive postures, 79
Downey Reflective Question, 43
five elements of, 67–72, 73–75
and follow-up conversations, 43, 52
framing questions, 85–97
and curriculum content, 87–90
expert teachers, 86–89
and instructional practices, 87–90
novice/apprentice teachers,
85–86, 87
professional teachers, 86
and indirect-independent
conversational sequences, 58–60
and instructional practices, 65, 72–73
and interdependent-direct approach,
60–75, 78–80
and supervisors, 79–80
taxonomy of
about, 90, 91–92
and curriculum content, 90, 95–96
and instructional practices, 90, 93–94
limitations of, 90, 97
and teachers, 79
of teachers, and Downey walk-
through, 3
and traditional supervisory practices, 80
and transformational thinking, 80
reflective learning environments,
collaborative, 139–40
reflective questions. *See* reflective inquiry
Reiman, A., 132, 134, 135, 137
relationships
and bureaucratic practices, xi,
160–62, 170
and classroom practices, xi
between employees and supervisors,
11–12, 45
between principals and teachers, ix, xi,
161–62, 166–70

professional, xi, 160–62, 170
between supervisors and teachers, 9
Remaley, A., 152
Ross-Gordon, J., 9, 132

safety and health issues, 21, 36
Sagor, R., 149, 154
Schaie, K., 134
Scholastic, Inc., 150
school culture. *See* educational cultures
scientific management, and supervisory
practices, x
Scriven, M., 152
Senge, P., 181
Simonton, D., 185
6th-grade mathematics scenario
and classroom walk-throughs, 37–38,
39–40
and notes, 47–48
and direct feedback statements
and record keeping, 106–7
and notes
and direct feedback statements, 51
Slack, P., 80
Slavin, R., 142
Smith, J., 149, 154
Soar, R., 152
Soder, R., 149, 154, 156
Steffy, B.
and deep alignment of curriculum,
26, 27, 31
and educational cultures, results
of changes in, 124
and teacher career development,
138, 176, 177, 178
Streshly, W., 130, 152
Stringfield, S., 149, 154
student(s)
and challenges and barriers to
change in educational cultures,
113–14
and MBWA, 149, 154
orientation to work, and five-step
observation informal
walk-throughs, 21–23
and preparations for classroom
walk-throughs, 101–2, 104
relationships with teachers, xi
superior-subordinate relationships, ix, x

supervisors
  and collaborative-interdependent
    reflective conversation, 76–77
  and collaborative reflective dialogue
    with teachers, 9
  and comfort level of teachers with, 22
  and direct feedback statements, 49
  and employee relationships, 11–12, 45
  and indirect-independent
    conversational sequences, 58–60
  and professional relationships, ix
  and reflective questions, 79–80
  supervisory practices of, ix–x
  and value of classroom
    walk-throughs, 7
  and working relationships with
    teachers, 9
supervisory practices. *See also* discursive
    practices
  and career cycle of teachers, 177–81
  clinical supervisory model, 132
  from corrective to discursive, 164–66
  developmental, 131–34
  "dipstick" model of supervision, xi
  and efficiency, x
  and evaluation issues, x, 10, 141–42,
    173, 174
  and gender discrimination, ix, x
  goal of, ix
  "gotcha" model of supervision, x–xi, 87
  and industrial models for interactions,
    x, 11–12
  and mentoring, 133
  and principals, ix–x, xi
  professionalization of, 126–31
  and scientific management, x
  and superior-subordinate relationships,
    ix, x
  and supervision of teachers, ix–x
  traditional, 160–61

Tanner, D., 126, 127, 128, 137
Tanner, L., 126, 127, 128, 137
taxonomy of reflective questions, 90,
    91–92
  and curriculum content, 90, 95–96
  and instructional practices, 90, 93–94
  limitations of, 90, 97
Taylor, Frederick, x

teachers. *See also* classroom practices;
    Management by Wandering Around
    (MBWA); novice/apprentice teachers
  actions of, 12
  as adult learners, 134–37
  and bureaucratic practices,
    xi, 160–62, 170
  career cycle of, 177–81
  classroom practice, and relationships
    with, xi
  and collaborative reflective dialogue
    with supervisors, 9
  comfort zone of, 22, 84–85, 84–87
  decisions by, 12–13
  and development of, 137–40
  and direct feedback statements, 49
  distinguished, 178
  efficiency issues, and supervision of, x
  emeritus, 178
  evaluation issues, and supervision of, x
  expert, 86, 87, 178
  and follow-up conversations with
    supervisors, 7–8
  growth of, 13, 175–85
    classroom walk-throughs and,
      176–77
    and feedback conversations,
      184–85
    organizational learning and
      transformation, 181–83
    and teacher career development,
      177–81
    transformative learning, 181
  Hunter model of teacher evaluation,
    10, 141–42
  and indirect reflective inquiry, 57
  and interactions with supervisors, 7–8
  isolates, and troubleshooting problems
    Downey walk-through model,
      172–73
  and lack of buy-in with Downey
    walk-through model, 171
  life cycle of career teacher model,
    177–81
  marginal, 114–16
  and normative gaze of principals,
    166–67
  and preparations for classroom
    walk-throughs, 101, 102–4

principal-teacher interactions, model
of, ix, xi, 161–62
professional, 86, 87, 178
and reflective conversations with
supervisors, 9
and reflective questions, 79, 84–85
and relationship with
supervisors/principals, ix, xi,
161–62, 166–70
self-analysis of, 13
troubleshooting problems with
Downey walk-through model,
171–73
and working relationships with
supervisors, 9
teaching effectiveness
and curriculum content, ix
Teddlie, C., 149, 154
Thies-Sprinthall, L., 132, 134,
135, 137
Thorndike, R., 27
Tileston, D., 154
traditional learning environments,
139–40
traditional supervisory practices, 80,
160–61
training seminars for classroom
walk-throughs, 108
Trueman, W., 144

12th-grade language arts scenario
and classroom walk-throughs, 18–20,
23, 26–32, 34
and direct feedback statements, 51
and notes, 47

Valentine, J. W., 149, 154
Villa, Susan, 123
Vygotsky, L., 137

Wagner, T., 110
Walker, D., 80, 184
"walk the walls"–curricular and
instructional decision, 21, 35–36
Waterman, R. Jr., 144
Watkins, K., 181
Webb, R., 28, 151
Weick, Karl, 182
Wells, H. G., 144
Welsh, Sue Wells, 10
West, G., 181
Whalen, S. P., 149
Wimpelberg, R., 149, 154
Wolfe, M., 138, 176, 177

Yorks, L., 181–82, 183

Zhu, N., 150
Zimmerman, D., 80

**CORWIN
PRESS**

The Corwin Press logo—a raven striding across an open book—represents the union of courage and learning. Corwin Press is committed to improving education for all learners by publishing books and other professional development resources for those serving the field of K–12 education. By providing practical, hands-on materials, Corwin Press continues to carry out the promise of its motto: **"Helping Educators Do Their Work Better."**